Going the Distance and Finishing Strong... by the Grace of God

Memories of a Seasoned Child of God

by Sally Power

xulon PRESS

TABLE OF CONTENTS

INTRODUCTION

I don't remember when I actually met Jean Yanakos. It seems she has always been a formidable voice in my spiritual journey. She was a part of the charismatic movement during the 70's – perhaps that's when I first heard her name. She spoke as one having authority and she had the personal experience to back it up!

Jean had a relationship with God the Father that you couldn't help but envy (it seems sacrilegious that a godly woman's life would inspire envy – perhaps a longing or hunger to emulate her life would be a more appropriate response!). Nonetheless, her relationship with the Father was intimate; they spent extensive time together, and He spoke to her – clearly, instructively, sharing revelations that she then taught to others with life-transforming power.

Years ago, I started prodding Jean to write a book about her life – I'm sure I was not the only one to suggest it! Anyone who heard her spiritual "adventures" wanted to review them and share them with others – and so the requests came – "You need to write a book!" "When are you going to write a book?" "Have you started the book yet?"

The thought of slowing down to organize her memoirs was not enticing to this maturing dynamo, so the project was waylaid, postponed, put on the back burner. She was simply too busy living to slow down to write! On Jean's recent 88th birthday (December 2010), I prodded AGAIN – "You've got to write a book!" Jean has never been one to shy away from expressing her opinion (as well as sharing promptings from the Holy Spirit), and she adamantly responded to my nudging.

"This is *my* revelation – not anyone else's. I don't want someone taking my revelation and turning it into something it's not supposed to be!"

I could appreciate that – I had walked long enough in the Christian community to see one person's "revelation" manipulated into a doctrine or dictate. I understood her concerns, but this was a life story that needed to be told!

"But your revelation is my *inspiration*," I countered.

With that response, she softened. "OK, if it provides inspiration for others, that would be good, but I don't have the time to do it." So I said to her, "For your birthday present, I will find you a ghostwriter!"

After some investigation, I realized the cost of securing a professional ghostwriter was prohibitive, yet I was deeply convinced that this was a project worth pursuing! During one of my morning walks, the divine inner voice prompted me – "Why not write the book yourself?" It was a huge leap of faith with a significant nudge from the Holy Spirit! And that is how the adventure began!

DEDICATED to

Jean's daughter, Carol

ACKNOWLEDGMENTS

Reflecting on my naiveté now, I can't help but chuckle! I had NO idea what I was committing myself to when I started this project. It required extensive audio taping, transcribing tapes into text, pouring over long-lost journals and notes, and compiling endless stories and revelations into some comprehensible order – a daunting task if I had any sense! However, Jean's life exemplifies moving beyond your comfort zone in response to God's leading – how appropriate that the writing of her memoires would require following that same example!

I told Jean that writing this book would take nine months because it takes nine months to birth a baby, and amazingly, it *has* taken nine months to complete this project.

I want to express my sincere thanks to many who have contributed to the "birthing" of this book:

To Jean for FINALLY agreeing to share her memoires and allowing me to spend time gleaning the information and pictures;

To Bob Tamasy for seasoned wisdom and advice in the writing process;

To Cindy Richey and Constance Pearson for hours of dedicated proofreading of manuscripts in various stages of completion;

To Suzanne Machek for editing expertise and direction;

To Don Priestley for much needed technical equipment and assistance, moral support, and manuscript submission; and

To many who offered prayers and words of encouragement for the completion of a book they believed in and desired to read!

But most of all, praise and thanksgiving to God Almighty – He stretches us beyond our own expertise and human strengths so that we may experience the amazing grace He has as He leads us on "adventures."

To God be the Glory!!! May this compilation of Jean's memories – her life and revelations – be *your* inspiration and cause you to desire to *go the distance* with Him!!

Blessings!
Sally Power

CHAPTER 1

IN THE BEGINNING

Carmella Panno lived in Manchester – a section of Pittsburgh, Pennsylvania, where many Italian immigrants resided. She had come to America when she was just seven years old; now she had seven children, and another one was on the way. The imminent birth was not met with joyful anticipation – one more mouth to feed! Her life was already difficult enough, washing infinite piles of laundry for her large family, cooking countless meals for her hungry brood, and scrubbing the wooden floors of their home with lye.

When her *comare* urged her to go to the bedroom for the birthing, she dismissed the words. She had too much to do – more to cook, more to clean, the children to take care of. Perhaps she even considered that she could avoid the unwelcomed "addition" if she postponed the event long enough. Her *comare* insisted she retreat to the bedroom, and Carmella continued to dismiss the urgings until the inevitable happened…

…unceremoniously Virginia Panno was born on the kitchen floor and wrapped in the newspaper that covered it!

As soon as I was born, the comare wrapped me up in the newspapers that were on the floor. Then she said these words, "For anyone to have such a hard birth, God must have His hand on her life in a special way." She prayed that I would become a missionary for God. She cupped my face in her hands and from that day forth, she would always call me her missionary. And that was how I was born.

The *comare* was someone very special, a significant person selected to share the most intimate moments of life - marriage, births, and funerals. This particular woman had numerous children of her own; she also had a husband who provided for their family. In contrast, Virginia's mother endured the responsibility of raising a family with little or no support from her husband. Her mother's *comare*, however, continued to affirm the call of God throughout Virginia's life. At every wedding and every funeral, she pulled Virginia aside and reminded her of her unique, God-ordained birthing. She would cup Virginia's face in her hands and proclaim, "You are my missionary. You are my missionary. Don't forget it."

Despite Virginia's divine birthing, her early life was filled with difficulties and hardship. When Virginia was three years old, her father left home with another woman who had her own family, abandoning his wife and eight growing children. The steadfast love and care of an earthly father was nonexistent in Virginia's early life.

Life during the Depression was – well, depressing. The lack of jobs and material goods often pressed people to desperate measures. Virginia's older brother became an alcoholic. When she was 4 years old, he molested her. She refused to tell anyone what had happened to her; it was an unspeakable source of shame.

In later years, my brother became a barber, and he generally had money, which he always kept in his pants pocket. When he was sleeping, I would steal the money from his pocket. When he woke up, he realized that the money was gone and would come to my school to get it back from me just to teach me a lesson. Years later, God showed me that I had robbed him because on a subconscious level I knew he had deeply robbed me!

Virginia had been violated by her "big" brother, someone who should have protected her and cared for her. The incident instilled an even greater longing for safety, security, and love.

Virginia had been named for her father's only sister. Her birth certificate identified her as "Virginia", but even at a very young age, Virginia was forthright and bold; she could discern a person's character and could express righteous indignation.

I was named after my father's sister, and I couldn't stand her. I didn't like her because her kids always had coffee and bread for breakfast. We used to go over there and watch her kids eat that coffee and bread as though it was something wonderful. She never offered us any coffee and never offered us any bread. We would stand there like little waifs, looking – staring – hoping that she would offer some bread. But she never did! When I was six years old, I said to my mother that I wanted my name changed. "I do not want to be called 'Virginia' anymore. I don't like her, and I don't want to be like her. So I want to change my name, and I want to be 'Jean'." Little did I know that "Jean" means "adored of God." Even then, God had His hand on my life, telling me what I should be called.

From that day forward, she was known as "Jean" to her family, friends, and new acquaintances. She did not formalize the name change with legal action because she was too young to pursue that and she did not have the finances. The name change, however, was irrefutable; she was "Jean".

In the early years of her life, Jean's family was desperately poor. She attended school every day in dresses made out of flour sacks marked with large, dark-inked XXs. Her mother was a skilled seamstress, and she would reconfigure the rough sack material into dresses secured with a ribbon and bow in the front. Every night her mother would hand wash the garment and hang it in the kitchen to dry; in the morning, Jean would put on the dried dress and set off for school. Despite the care and provision that her mother creatively provided, the dress was a blatant reminder of her impoverished status.

All the kids would make fun of me because I dressed differently from anyone else. Even at that age, I hated that dress made out of a flour sack, but now I realize that it was a way that I was set apart from everyone else. No one else had a dress that had XXs on it because it was a flour sack. I wore flour sack dresses until I was about 10 years old. It was very humbling, but God knew that was what I needed.

Jean's life was not filled with abundant provision. Her mother did not have the means to provide luxuries for her children; she barely had enough to provide basic daily foods. As the children became older, they also contributed to the family income. Two of her brothers were barbers, and her sister worked for the WPA, Roosevelt's recovery program to provide jobs during the Depression. Her sister's income did much to maintain the family. Jean's mother worked three jobs: cleaning houses, taking in washing and ironing, and baking bread.

My mother's married name – my maiden name – was "Panno". In Italian that means "bread maker". My mother made 24 loaves of bread a day. During the Depression, that's how we lived; I sold bread every day. I would go door to door selling bread. It was tough during the Depression.

At Christmas time we never had toys. I was 12 years old before I ever got anything for Christmas - then, I got a set of tin dishes. That was the only Christmas gift that I ever remember getting. But my mother would bake. She would make special Italian delicacies that were really good! That was the emphasis of our Christmas. Those little cookies made out of dates and nuts I still remember...and there was an apple and an orange. That was our Christmas.

In later years, when Jean reflected on her upbringing, she was tempted to engage in a "pity party" because hers was a difficult childhood. During one particular melancholy recollection, God led her to Psalm 139, confirming that He had established her life:

Psa 139:1-13 To the choirmaster. A Psalm of David. O LORD, you have searched me and known me! (2) You know when I sit down and when I rise up; you discern my thoughts from afar. (3) You search out my path and my lying down and are acquainted with all my ways. (4) Even before a word is on my tongue, behold, O LORD, you know it altogether. (5) You hem me in, behind and before, and lay your hand upon me. (6) Such knowledge is too wonderful for me; it is high; I cannot attain it. (7) Where shall I go from your Spirit? Or where shall I flee from your presence? (8) If I ascend to heaven, you are there! If I make my bed in Sheol, you are there! (9) If I take the wings of the morning and dwell in the uttermost parts of the sea, (10) even there your hand shall lead me, and your right hand shall hold me. (11) If I say, "Surely the darkness shall cover me, and the light about me be night," (12) even the darkness is not dark to you; the night is bright as the day, for darkness is as light with you. (13) For you formed my inward parts; you knitted me together in my mother's womb.

See – this is amazing...while I was covered in my mother's womb and then being birthed on the floor, it was the Lord who covered me.

Psa 139:14-16 I praise you, for I am fearfully and wonderfully made. Wonderful are your works; my soul knows it very well. (15) My frame was not hidden from you, when I was being made in secret, intricately woven in the depths of the earth. (16) Your eyes saw my unformed substance; in your book were written, every one of them, the days that were formed for me, when as yet there was none of them.

In other words even before my days were fashioned, God knew what was coming down the pike.

Psa 139:17-24 How precious to me are your thoughts, O God! How vast is the sum of them! (18) If I would count them, they are more than the sand. I awake, and I am still with you. (19) Oh that you would slay the wicked, O God! O men of blood, depart from me! (20) They speak against you with malicious intent; your enemies take your name in vain! (21) Do I not hate those who hate you, O LORD? And do I not loathe those who rise up against you? (22) I hate them with complete hatred; I count them my enemies. (23) Search me, O God, and know my heart! Try me and know my thoughts! (24) And see if there be any grievous way in me, and lead me in the way everlasting!

I can go back to that and say, "Okay, I was born when I was supposed to be born and how I was supposed to be born. I wore what I was supposed to wear. I wore paper first, but now I have beautiful clothes that God has provided. I had a humble birth, yet I know it was a supernatural birth and I know that I was destined for God." As I look back on the path of my life, I know that I was destined to be something for God. And the older I get, the more I know that that is true…I know God's hand is upon me.

With the Depression forming the backdrop of her adolescent years, Jean grew into an attractive young woman. She entertained herself with simple pleasures that did not require spending money that her family did not have, such as going for walks, buying a nickel ice cream cone at the corner drug store, dancing at the local beer gardens, and playing cards – all kinds of cards. As Jean navigated through her teen years, she began to explore the typical "boy meets girl" attraction, and she met young men of interest through family and friends.

I had a cousin, and we were very, very close. She was never able to get a boyfriend. She was nice enough, but not striking as far as beauty in shape or anything like that. There was a neighbor who lived next to my cousin. He was interested in my cousin, but she was not interested in him. He asked if he could bring a friend down so we could double date, but she wanted the friend for herself.

When the friend came down with this next-door neighbor, my cousin saw him and she said to me, "Don't look at him! Don't talk to him! Because when he sees you, he'll never look at me!" That was like throwing a bone to a dog! I immediately made up my mind that I was going to get him away from her – no matter what!

The "friend" fell in love with Jean immediately. He was attractive and charming, but he also had a drinking problem. Jean had no idea about that! During their courtship, they would spend time together, having coffee and talking; he would drop her off at her home at the specified hour – she was required to be home by a certain curfew. Jean was unaware that he would then go out with his friends and spend half the night drinking. When he arrived home intoxicated, his mother assumed that he had spent the entire evening with Jean. Consequently, his mother did not have a very high opinion of Jean.

I got married when I was 19 years of age. My husband was in the service in South Carolina. I got on the bus by myself; my mother let me go to South Carolina on the Fourth of July. He had already made arrangements in the little town called Lexington. He found a justice of the peace, and we went into her office. She married us, and he asked her how much it was. She said, "Whatever you want to give," because there was no set charge. He gave her three dollars, and I was a little upset. We were short on money; three dollars was a lot of money! And he said, "Don't you think it was worth three dollars?" I couldn't say anything to that, although later I could've questioned it.

During the first two years of marriage, Jean's husband was stationed in South Carolina. Jean would save money for visitations. That was when she began to realize that he drank excessively.

I would go to visit him in South Carolina. I would save enough money to go down there and stay for two or three weeks, and then I would come back home and save enough money to go again. That's when I saw that he had started to drink. An officer in the Army wrote a book about their division. In the book, he described my husband's life in the Army, and how he would go AWOL to get drunk. He would be gone for two or three weeks. When he came back, they didn't throw him in jail because he was an expert marksman. He could shoot with such clarity. He was so good at it that they wouldn't throw him in jail. They should've!

He began to gamble while he was in the Army, and he began to pick up all the other tricks that go with drinking. I don't know how many women, and I didn't ask him. I never asked him, "Well, did you go out or did you do this or did you do that?" I felt he was in sin, and it didn't matter. I decided I didn't want to know about the past.

During World War II, Jean's husband served overseas for almost four years. When he was discharged after the war, the young couple settled in Pittsburgh to be near both of their families.

Her husband was startled when Jean's brother took her to the train station to greet him upon discharge. He had not planned on going directly to his home. Instead of returning home with his young bride, he went to his mother's residence and began a drinking binge that continued for a month. Jean rarely knew where he was.

His drinking problems had surfaced prior to being in the service, but after experiencing the ravages of war, the problems intensified. Jean hardly recognized this person who had returned. Today his symptoms would be classified as post-traumatic stress, but at that time it was only seen as terrifying. The relationship became more tumultuous; Jean's husband was demanding and controlling. When he was drinking, he became "a nasty drunk" – aggressive and irrational.

He would get drunk, and if he didn't like something – say you had a dish on the table – he wouldn't say anything. He'd just pick up the dish and break it. If he finished eating a bowl of spaghetti and I didn't clean up right away, he'd just throw it up at the ceiling. You never knew what he was going to do. He was a very violent man.

When he was not drinking, their relationship was pleasant enough; over the next few years, they had two children. When he drank, which became more and more frequent, there was a barrage of physical and verbal abuse; he would chase Jean around the house and beat her. He would throw her out of the house, or she would run out on her own volition to escape.

The years went by and the abuse continued. Once Jean was running from him, and her daughter was running with her. Her husband chased after Jean and tried to run over her with his car!

Jean's daughter Carol saved her mother's life many times! When Jean was staying with her sister, Jean and her daughter were cleaning up the basement which served as their make-shift dining room. Jean's husband, in one of his violent rages, climbed in through the basement window in pursuit of her.

That window was only maybe 2 feet high. I don't know how he didn't get stuck in there. He grabbed me by the throat and was choking me! Carol got up on his back and started hitting him and kept biting him and scratching him until he stopped. That's how she saved my life because I was already passing out from him strangling me.

The familiar pattern continued, and her husband's drinking escalated. When he was drunk, Jean was never certain what to expect regarding his behavior, and she often did not know where he was. He would disappear for two or three weeks at a time – sometimes even months. His gambling increased, and their life became even more chaotic.

He would get enough money together – say $10,000 – and he would go to Las Vegas. He would go in his greasy work clothes and ride first class. Can you believe that? He would call us when he was coming home, and we would meet the plane. Each one of us would be hiding behind a pillar because when he came off the plane, we didn't want people to know that he belonged to us because he looked so terrible. He was drunk – he was in greasy work clothes – but he didn't care! When you're drunk, you don't know and you don't care. Of course, he would lose all the money. There was nothing! Money was always hard to come by.

Jean's family had a low opinion of her husband; her mother and sister were repeatedly providing financial support for food, clothing, and shelter for Jean and her family because her husband was squandering their meager funds. They would frequently say, "You don't have to put up with that; you can

21

always come home." Jean would retreat to her mother's home with her two children, but that home was not a peaceful paradise. Her siblings had returned to her mother's homestead with their children, and often there were as many as 14 people living within a 6-room residence. The chaos of that existence was not tolerable either.

It was one of those Catch-22 situations – I didn't have a place to stay, so I always had to go back. It would be fine for a couple days, and then it would be the same thing over again. It was just repetitive because any time he got drunk, he was a very nasty, mean drunk. You know when some people drink, they get happy. He was never a happy camper. And that was what happened.

Jean rationalized that it was not her husband's fault; he had grown up in a very bad neighborhood with numerous houses of prostitution around his home. He witnessed prostitutes having sex in the middle of the streets and on top of cars; because of this, he believed that women were objects to be used. He had no regard for their worth in general.

His mother was not very helpful, as far as helping him to understand loving a woman. His mother was so hard on him. She threw him out when he was 15 years old, and he slept in the park for two years. How can you do that as a Christian – throw your kid out in the street?

Jean struggled with her marriage; it was intolerable. She was concerned for her husband and wanted a better life, but how could that be? She was desperate to seek help for him. Hope came from her husband's mother, despite her harshness toward her son in his teen years. His mother and his sister demonstrated a devout belief in God.

My mother-in-law and my sister-in-law were Christians, and so they would witness to me all the time. I would get down and pray with them, but I really didn't know what I was doing. I did it to please them really. Then my mother-in-law invited me to church and she said, "If you come to church, your husband will come with you." I knew he needed to be saved, so I went to church with her and him. I do not know how she ever got him to agree to that, but he came to church. When they gave the altar call, I went forward. I kept looking back for him, but he wasn't following me. By this time, there were so many people coming up that I couldn't go back to my seat.

Jean continued to the altar, pressed by the lack of an escape route more than a desire to personally repent. Her motivation was to help her husband. He was so miserable; their marriage was so miserable. If going to the altar could make things better, then that's what she would do!

So I went on up to the altar. That was the first time I heard the voice of God within my own spirit. I was weeping and crying that my husband would get saved. Then I heard a voice within me saying, "It's you that is standing in the need of prayer." I turned around and I saw an elderly woman behind me. I said, "Excuse me, what did you say?" She said, "I didn't say anything."

I turned back to the altar, and I started praying for my husband again. I heard again, "It's you that's standing in the need of prayer. It's you that could go to hell." I turned around and said, "Excuse me, what did you say?" The woman said again, "I didn't say a word, but the next time you hear that, say, 'Speak, Lord, your servant hears.

I went back to praying again. Then I realized it <u>was</u> me standing in the need of prayer! I was a Catholic, and I never knew that I could be a candidate for hell! So I said, "Lord, if this is you – if this is <u>really</u> You, then speak to my heart." And He did! He said, "I want you as My child." I said, "I don't know what that means, but I want to be Your child." Truthfully, I didn't really feel anything.

Jean attended the Assemblies of God Church that her in-laws attended. Within her difficult life circumstances, God was her only hope. She found comfort through reading the Bible and in God's Presence, but the teaching she received from the church leaders was often harsh and condemning.

We were taught that divorce was out of the question. I remember going to my pastor and telling him what I was going through. I was told that you called your husband "lord".

There is a scripture in the Old Testament where Sarah called Abraham "lord", and that's what my pastor said. "Call him 'lord' and be totally submissive to him." And I said, "Yeah, when he beats me up and he's trying to kill me?" and he said, "Yeah, just call him 'lord'." And I said, "There's something wrong with this teaching!"

Jean refused to embrace the distorted teachings of unconditional submission, yet because of her deep commitment to her Christian faith, she also did not consider divorce. Caught between a rock and a hard place, she would retreat to alternative living situations to make life bearable for her and her children.

We separated back and forth a hundred times. It was a love-hate relationship. I couldn't stand to live with him, and he couldn't stand to live without me. I would leave and go to my mother's, and then he would start calling me and saying, "Come on home. I'm sorry. I'll never touch you again."

This repetitive pattern continued for many years. Her children grew up and established homes of their own, but Jean continued in the toxic cycle of her dysfunctional marriage. Finally, the abuse and uncertainty became too much, and Jean moved out. There were those within the Christian church who did not sanction the separation, but she felt a peace with God that for her sanity, safety and very life, she needed to leave.

Her Christian life did not resemble that of other churchgoers she knew. Her life was unconventional and unique; nonetheless God was a reality in her life. Despite all that had happened – an uncelebrated birth, abandonment by her father, and an abusive, alcoholic husband – Jean STILL knew God had a purpose and a plan for her life – to give her a future and a hope. God, and God alone, was her security through it all – even when it made no natural sense.

CHAPTER 2

THE CALL OF GOD

In the midst of her abusive marriage, perhaps even because of it, Jean drew closer to God. She wanted a life that showed His love and truth and peace. As the loving father that Jean had never known, God the Father began teaching Jean a better way to live; He revealed that past actions could be stumbling blocks, and they needed to be addressed. He began to teach life lessons to His child.

When I was a young girl I worked in a candy store, one of the most famous candy stores in our city. This company was famous for their Easter eggs and creams. People would order them from all over the country, and we mailed them out every day all over the world. Employees were not allowed to eat any of the candy without paying for it. For me that was like true torture; I loved chocolate, especially the raspberry cream or fruit and nut eggs! I couldn't pay for the candy because I never would have any money, so I began mailing myself 5 or 10 pound chocolate eggs or boxes of candy because they never checked the mail orders. I worked there for over a year.

Then I got married, and I became a Christian. Shortly afterwards, as I began to spend time in prayer, I would see all this candy I had stolen. I kept rebuking the devil for tormenting me. Finally, it dawned on me that this could be the Holy Spirit showing me that I needed to make it right.

Jean considered going to her former employer and having a face-to-face confession, but the embarrassment of such a confrontation was unbearable. She postponed dealing with any confession or restitution, but that too was unbearable – each time she attempted to pray she involuntarily visualized that mountain of candy. The dilemma would not resolve itself; she resigned to the fact that she would have to take some action.

I thought I would write her a letter. I picked out the most beautiful card and wrote my story to her [the former employer]. I shared how I had become a Christian and God had forgiven me for my sin, but I needed to ask her for her forgiveness for stealing the candy. At the time, I was very hard-pressed as far as finances, but I wrote that I would be willing to work for her in her room or at the office, but not in the candy store because I knew I would be tempted again.

The letter went out. Three weeks later, I received a beautiful card from her with her response, "If God forgave you, so do I." The sad thing is that three weeks later she committed suicide by drinking carbonic acid. I believe if I had not asked for forgiveness, I would be bound to her by guilt. So my life lesson is when I feel the least bit of conviction, I immediately try to make right what God is dealing with me about.

Jean's spiritual education continued; as the next step of Christian growth, Jean's sister-in-law and other women in her church encouraged her to receive the Holy Spirit. Jean didn't even know there was a Holy Spirit! She had attended the Catholic Church all her life, but to the best of her recollection, she had never heard teachings about the Third Person of the Trinity. Regardless of her ignorance or skepticism, she trusted these women, and if there was additional empowerment that God would pour out to enable her to live more fully for Him, she wanted it!

"What do I do?"

"You raise your hands and start praising the Lord."

The instructions were simplistic; however, there was one personal complication - for seven years Jean had worn a back brace prescribed by her doctor to correct a severe injury caused from falling down the steps. The brace was a formidable contraption consisting of 26 steel ribs with straps that secured in the front. Once fastened, it was so constricting that Jean's back was ramrod straight and movement was significantly limited. She could not bend in any direction; she could only walk absolutely upright. It was the last thing she took off at night and the first thing she put on in the morning.

I trusted the women who were praying with me. It was funny because some of their prayers were "Lord, send the fire." I thought that sounded like a good idea. Then another person would say, "Send the rain tonight." That sounded like a good idea, too, but won't it put the fire out? I got so confused that I had to tune them out. Finally, I said, "Lord, if this is of You, then You let it happen. I don't need any help from them. I want everything from You." And so with that, I raised my hands, and without realizing it, I fell backwards. When I fell backwards, I heard my sister-in-law saying, "She must be receiving a healing or she would not be able to do that." And then I said, "Lord, I'll take it." Because I didn't even know there was such a thing as divine healing! I kept moving back and forth kind of rocking, and I kept saying, "If that's of You, I take it! I receive it!" When I got up, I felt like my feet never touched the ground! I went home absolutely like I was floating on air.

That night when Jean arrived home, she took off her brace as she had done so many times before, but she never put it on again! Her back was healed, and she was immersed into a deeper understanding of God's grace and goodness.

Jean longed to be in the house of the Lord, and she insisted her children go along with her. Since she had no car, the trip to church was made via public transportation; public transportation required street car tokens. Her two young children could ride for free, but her fare was a prerequisite for getting to church.

I wanted to go to church so bad. I had such a hunger to go to church because I didn't know anything and I wanted to learn as much as I could. I had no money whatsoever – not even a dime! I took my two kids – I dragged them everywhere with me! I had one kid on one hip and one on the other hip, and we were walking up the street. We lived on a steep street that was a 45° angle, and I was dragging myself up the street with my two kids. There was snow almost to my knees - that's how deep the snow was!

Finally, we came to a place in the road, and you could go right or left. I decided to go right. When I had just gotten past that fork in the street, I looked down and right on the edge of the street there was a quarter lying on top of the snow. Now you know how heavy a quarter is – it should have gone down and I should've never seen it! But it was like somebody laid it on top of the snow, and I could see it immediately! It shone, and I grabbed it. I said, "Oh, praise God! I can get three tokens to go to church now!" because you could get 3 tokens for quarter.

I had that quarter in my hand, and I was just praising God and saying, "Thank you, Lord!" I got up to the streetcar stop, got my three tokens, and we got to church. I knew once I got to church someone would always offer us a ride home; it was getting to church that was a problem.

Jean used her provisional tokens for three weeks, and then she was in the same dilemma – no money and no transportation for church. Remembering how God had provided before, she started to take the same route and looked for a quarter to be provided in the same way. Then she had a change of heart.

I was going to go the same route, like most of us do when God does something one way, but I changed my mind. I took the other road as I was going up. On the other road, I found a half a dollar lying on top of the snow. You know, a half dollar is heavier than a quarter! If someone lost it, it would go down into the snow, and I wouldn't be able to see it. But it was laying there like someone had put it on top – like someone had placed it on the snow just perfectly. I stopped right away and picked it up. I was so excited because this meant six tokens, and I'd be able to go to church six times!

Again Jean marveled at the providential provision and enjoyed six weeks of secured transportation. God was truly her Provider, and she was growing in her confidence of being His child. What would happen when this supply was used up? Would His resources continue?

After six weeks, I ran out of those tokens. I went up to the corner and waited, hoping someone would be going by that I knew. Maybe someone would be going into the Northside and could give me a ride. I was standing there with my kids, and I was praying and praying and praying. I said, "Oh, God, I want go to church so bad!" I knew if I didn't take the next streetcar coming, there was no use in going because it would be too late. If I didn't get that streetcar, I would have to turn around to go back home – there is no way I wanted to go back home!

I did something that I thought would give me a heart attack; I got on the street car with my two kids. I had not a dime in my pocket, and I got on the streetcar! There was no one on there – not a soul. I walked back to the next of the last seat, and I put the kids there. Then I went to the very last seat to sit down. There was a dollar bill! It was placed; there was not a wrinkle on it! If it had come out of someone's pocket, it would've had wrinkles on it, but it was right there – right on the seat. I picked it up and I thought, "Oh, God!"

That was the end of me ever worrying about money. I knew God was always going to supply for me. He proved it to me – each time He doubled the amount! I learned then that when you trust God, He's going to provide His blessing when you walk in faith. Well, at that time, I don't know if you would call it faith – it was just such a desire – a hunger – because I wanted to learn. I was just a new babe in Christ, and I didn't know much of anything.

There were other ways that God provided for Jean and her family. Jean's husband was strict regarding any expenditures; she had to account for every dime she spent on groceries, and whatever funds were not used she had to give back to him. The allotment was hardly enough to feed the family of four, but God made a way.

I would go to the store and when I would walk in the grocer would say to me," I have a whole basket of bananas and apples here. Can you use them?" I would say to myself, "Does a bear sleep in the woods?" There were other times when people brought us Thanksgiving dinner and I would die because I knew my husband was going to have a fit! He said, "What are you telling these people? Are you telling them that you don't have enough food to eat?" I would say, "No, Bill. It's God that's doing it." God provided for me in so many different ways!

Inspired by God's provision, Jean continued seeking God for spiritual provision, too. One morning she began her daily devotions in the book of Samuel. She had read about Eli, the old prophet of God. In that passage, the young boy Samuel had heard his name being called, and Samuel thought it was Eli. Samuel went to Eli.

"What do you want? Why are you calling me?" he asked Eli.

Eli explained that he had not called the boy and Eli sent him back. The whole thing happened again - three times! Finally, it dawned on Eli that this must be God speaking to this young boy.

"The next time you hear that voice, say, 'Lord, your servant hears," instructed Eli.

I had just read the passage that morning, and then I heard my name being called three times "Jean! Jean! Jean!" It reverberated, and I was scared to death! I thought, "What am I getting into? Is this weird? Is this the devil?" I didn't know! I couldn't differentiate between God and the devil because I never heard anything like that before. So I took the chance, and I said, "Speak for your servant hears." And He said, "Heal the sick."

Jean was not easily convinced! This proclamation seemed so irrational that she could not believe it was truly from God. To occupy her mind, she picked up the Sunday school quarterly, a small notebook-size pamphlet. As the Sunday school teacher for the eight-year-old boys in her church, she often referenced this booklet. On the front page was a picture of Jesus. Above the picture were the words "His Ministry" and underneath the picture it said "… to teach, preach, and heal the sick." The words were so profound and seemed to confirm her "calling".

My thought was that sounds pretty good, so I said, "Okay, Lord, I receive that." Then doubt began. You have no education; you have no money; your husband is not saved; you've got small children to take care of… all these arguments.

He spoke to my heart again and said, "I want you to turn to Matthew 10." I barely knew where Matthew was, so I started flipping through the Bible, and finally, I found it. This was where Jesus sent them out two by two, and they went into every city teaching and preaching and healing. That was a pretty good confirmation. But then I began to doubt again - God doesn't call women, you have no education, how are you going to learn the Bible – on and on and on and on. All these thoughts whirled in my mind. So finally I said, "God, please don't get angry, but could You reveal to me one more time? If You reveal to me one more time, then I promise You, I will not ask You again."

So this time, I turned to Luke 6. I didn't know that Matthew, Mark, and Luke are synoptic Gospels. In other words, what you read in one, you will also read in another. So I turned to Luke 9:6 "And they departed and went through the villages, preaching the gospel and healing everywhere." And I said, "Okay, Lord, but I'm not going to tell anyone that you've called me to preach."

Jean briefly enjoyed her false sense of anonymity, thinking that her "secret" was secure. She pondered it within her own heart…but she did share it with one person, her best friend. This woman was her steadfast prayer partner. Each morning they would gather in her best friend's home from 10:00AM until noon to pray; on Saturday and Sunday they were in church together. This was a trusted confidante. When Jean confided what had transpired, her friend was amused.

"I don't know why you're arguing because you've been doing that all along - you're already praying, you've already been teaching, and you've already been preaching!"

Soon after her "calling", a special meeting was held at the church Jean was attending, and a visiting evangelist conducted the service. His sermon was deeply inspiring, and the woman in front of Jean started spinning around and around in joyous response to the message. Without bumping into the pew, she continued spinning, and then stopped abruptly. Instead of facing forward at the speaker, the woman was facing the back and stared directly at Jean.

She said, "You've been called to preach, and I want you to preach at my church." I looked at her and I said, "What?" And then I felt a hand on my shoulder, and I heard in my ear, "I have opened the first door for you."

The woman attended an Afro-American congregation located in Homestead, Pennsylvania. Jean and her white-haired secretary had to take two streetcars to navigate to the obscure location. The missionary meeting was already in progress when the women entered the building, and the congregation was worshipping and praising the Lord. The meeting seemed to continue forever; it dragged on and on and on. Jean repeatedly glanced at her watch because she knew when her children were expected home from school. Finally, Jean was invited to the podium. Shortly after she commenced speaking, a woman stood up and said, "My name is Daisy May. The Lord woke me up this morning and said, 'Daisy May, I have got a blessing for you. You go down to the church, and I will let you know when the just blessing comes.' I've been down here all day waiting for the blessing, and the blessing hasn't come until this woman stood up and started to give her testimony."

And with that, the power of God touched this woman, and she began to run all over the whole church. She scared me half to death! I'd never seen anything like that before in my whole life. And while she's running all around praising the

Lord, the other people began to just praise and dance and sing.

I moved to the back of the church at the wall. I said to the pastor of that church, "I had <u>nothing</u> to do with this!" Because by this time, they were running, some were jumping, some were singing, some were dancing...I mean stuff that I'd never seen before! Bedlam is all I can think of. It was bedlam!

That was my first time preaching, and the power of God came down and people were touched everywhere. I kept saying to the pastor, "I had nothing to do with it. Nothing! Nothing! Nothing!" I didn't! I didn't have anything to do with it! It was just the power of God that had come down, and I never forgot that. All my life I never forgot that first time, and I couldn't even tell anybody because I knew no one would ever believe that that would ever happen!

God had a purpose and a plan and Jean was eager to be part of it. She began opening her home for prayer meetings. Soon about 70 to 100 people were coming on a regular basis each week. There were three who emerged as preachers in this impromptu congregation, Jean and two men. They alternated in their teaching and preaching, and the threesome developed an effective ministry. It seemed to be the beginning of a tri-fold ministry, but God had a different plan in mind, specifically for Jean.

I had a vision, and I saw three huge shocks of wheat. I saw the shepherd's crook take one shock away and then another. I saw the one left in the middle, and I heard in my spirit, "This is your stock of wheat, and it was not taken away.

Jean continued to grow in her ministry of "preaching, teaching and healing the sick." Jean became the pastor of a small congregation in Bellevue. For the first 5 years, they met in the local YMCA. When a vacated church building became available in Beechview, Pennsylvania, they bought it. Jean pastored that small church called Calvary Pentecostal Church for 32 years. It was a modest but enthusiastic congregation. As part of that ministry, she established tent meetings and traveled from town to town in the western Pennsylvania region, ministering to those who were hungry for God's presence.

First, Jean would preach a stirring message; then prayer lines would form and she prayed for various needs. If the first prayer recipient fell down under the power of God, Jean noted that the whole line would do the same. They remained down for only a few seconds, and Jean questioned the authenticity of their actions.

I knew I had the power of God in my life, but…I knew that wasn't God. I begin to admonish them: if they went down, they had to stay there until God was through dealing with them. It was amazing how many didn't go down!

We are like - I hate to use these words but - dumb sheep. I'm afraid that's about what it amounts to! We either follow what others do or say or go off on our own and have to have the shepherd rescue us because we either get lost or worse. Some of my greatest lessons of life have been when I have been wounded, sick, or in distress, and I had to be put down on my bed. Then I learned to hear His voice. Activity was taken away from me, and I learned my dependence was on Him.

Jean learned stories of how the wayward little sheep went his own rebellious way and was injured. The shepherd then carried that sheep on his shoulders. The little sheep was fed dainties and berries that the other sheep are not privy to, and because of his self-imposed isolation, he learned to recognize that shepherd's voice. In sheep countries, several flocks are driven into the mountains to graze at the same time. At the end of the grazing time, the shepherd begins to call his sheep, and no matter how many flocks are there, the sheep know their shepherd's voice.

That's what He means when He says, "My sheep know my voice and another they will not follow." Are we willing to let Him do as it says in Psalm 23:2, "He makes me lie down in green pastures…."? Are we able to lay everything down and enter into a true rest? In Hebrews 4:9-10, the Scripture says, "So then, there remains a Sabbath rest for the people of God, (10) for whoever has entered God's rest has also rested from his works as God did from his." So many times it is such hard work because we want to carry our own load and wonder why we are so weary and heavy laden. We are so used to being in control! It's hard to let go and let God do it.

Intimacy with God naturally revealed the amazing power of God. As Jean studied God's Word, she became convinced that healing was for now. She began to pray in faith that the infirmed would be healed because this aligned with what the Scriptures stated. As those who were suffering with severe illness or disease came to Jean, she prayed in faith believing – and one by one the recipients of her prayers...died! Not just one or two – several!

It finally got to the place where people would say, "Don't let Jean pray for you because you KNOW what happens - everyone she prays for dies!" It became very discouraging! This continued for two years and frankly began to shake my faith in healing...to shake my faith in my own faith. I thought, "Okay, I will go through the motions of praying", but I really didn't have any faith whatsoever.

The season of seemingly unanswered prayers came to an end. Jean's faith was restored, and God released His power in fuller measure. She preached the Gospel and taught the grace and goodness of God to those who came for prayer, having His Presence confirmed with signs of healing and pro-phetic words. Jean was fully aware that all the glory and power belonged to God, but sometimes people mistakenly idolized the messenger rather than the awesome Source!

In the late 1960s, tent meeting revivals were held in the little town of Homer City, Pennsylvania. During that time, 500 people came to the Lord and were baptized in a nearby muddy creek. God continued to confirm His power with "signs and wonders". One evening the ministry continued long into the evening. Jean, a humble but human servant, was exhausted! Some women approached her and asked her to pray for their friend who was dying of cancer.

Jean's inner cry and audible groan sighed "I'm too tired!" And she thought to herself, "Would Jesus have said that?!?"

"But we drove over 80 miles to get here!"

Reluctantly, Jean followed the persistent bearers to a spot under a tree where they had left their friend reclining. Even trudging up the grade to the tree, Jean's legs felt like lead weights. The party of women arrived at the bed of the infirmed man. He was emaciated – a skeleton with skin loosely wrapped around it! Jean admitted that her prayer was bland and seemingly uninspired.

"Lord, put some meat on his bones and heal him." That was it; she staggered down the hillside and went home to rest.

Several months later, Jean was ministering again at another revival meeting in Homestead. Petitioners waited patiently in long lines for prayer. Jean looked up at the next person seeking a touch from God, and she saw a hefty man with a generous belly bulging over his belt.

"Do you remember me?" he asked. I hate when people ask me that, but I didn't say so. I just said, "No I'm sorry. I don't believe I do." "I'm the man who was dying of cancer, and you prayed that God would put some meat on my bones and now look at me!" So I said to him, "Well, it looks like God did just that. Is that what you came to tell me?" And he said, "No, now I want you to pray that He takes some off – look at me, I'm fat!"

Jean capitalized on the opportunity to teach about personal discipline and being a steward of your body, the Temple of the Holy Spirit. What a sense of humor God demonstrated - He used a weary saint to demonstrate His healing power, and then He presented a teachable moment to refine one of His children!

God made a place for Jean as she steadfastly followed His leadings. Her heart's desire was to proclaim God's goodness and never to distort the truth - all the glory belonged to Him! Jean had a radio program on station WPIT, 730 on the dial. The program was broadcast throughout the Pittsburgh and tri-state area, and it continued on the air from 1954 to 1976.

She purposely did not use her own name in the title. Instead, she entitled the program *Jesus and Me*, using an inclusive personal pronoun that any listener could replace with his or her own name. Intentionally, Jean had selected a name that was not self-promoting because her heart's intent was to lift up the name of Jesus, not Jean Yanakos. She did not use her personal photographs, even when listeners requested that she send one. An enterprising businessman from Ohio approached Jean with a contrary agenda.

He said, "If you would let me be your PR man, I can make you a by-word across the state." I wasn't about to have him make me a household word. I told him, "If God doesn't lift me up, I don't want man to." And that was that – I wasn't really well-known or popular, but then that wasn't my intention.

Jean was also adamant in her belief that if God had called her to a ministry, He would supply the finances. She was appalled by the dramatic pleas from other radio stations lamenting, "If you don't supply this need, we'll have to go off the air." According to her strong opinion, if God ordained a ministry, it was His responsibility to provide the resources to maintain it. Subsequently, if God no longer supplied the need through whatever means He chose, it was no longer His Will to continue the ministry.

For years, her mother's *comare* sent her a dollar a week in envelopes addressed without a specific name, simply "To My Missionary." Jean always marveled that the dollar reached her! This on-going provision through her precious family friend demonstrated God's steadfast care for Jean; she was His child! When the financial resources for her program dried up, Jean closed the doors on her radio program without fanfare or an elaborate explanation. She was content to seek God's next mission for her life.

About the same time, the Lord also directed Jean to leave the church she was pastoring. He made clear that His purpose was for the growth and health of His entire flock, and if that required some intense pruning, so be it!

He said. "You do this people a disservice because they come here and they only want you to tickle their ears. They want you to teach them. You do everything - you do the teaching, you do the praying, you do the fasting, you even clean the church. They are content to just sit and soak it up, but they don't want Me to squeeze them out."

God dealt with me for about six months before I finally said to them, "This is the last Sunday I'll be here in this church. We're to close the doors, and that's it." As a result of me doing that, all were scattered. They became teachers and pastors; they became elders to build up other churches. So you see, by me keeping them there with me, they were actually stunted in their growth!

Yet again, God showed His faithfulness by giving direction for the good of the Body of Christ – and for the good of Jean. He was demonstrating His purpose and calling through an imperfect vessel – Jean – and through that process, He was refining her, too!

So God does call women, even women with unsaved husbands without an education – Amen and amen!

For a season, God closed the doors of direct ministry, such as her radio program and small congregation, but His provision and direction for Jean continued. One of the congregants from her church, a young woman who had worked at the church for Jean, had a small juice bar business at the European Health Spa (where the current Club Julian is located). The young woman was unable to maintain her business and offered to sell it to Jean for the price of the inventory.

So I bought it for $400. I would make soup and protein drinks, and that's how it started to be built up. The owner of the club was charging her $275 a month for rent – it was deplorable! The equipment was horrible; they had not done anything to it for about 30 years. I went to the manager and said, "I'm afraid I may have to give this up." He said, "Why?" I said, "I'm not making enough money to pay the rent. I can come up here and spend every day working and not make any money." So the manager said to his boss, "Why are we charging her anything? Let her have it for nothing. She doesn't have to pay any rent – she's doing our clients a service by being here."

I was there for eight years and never paid a dime's rent. I made a lot of money while I was there – that's how I was able to survive. It was amazing, and I would minister to the people who came.

Jean worked every Sunday at the juice bar, which limited her attendance at other churches. Then she heard of a relatively new church, Northway Christian Community founded by Jay Passavant and his wife and several other couples who were seeking meaningful fellowship following God. The congregation met in an old restaurant building, and she decided to check it out. A guest speaker presented the message, but Jean quickly discerned that this was a "good" church that was hungry for the power of God.

The following week the air conditioner broke down at the spa; patrons stopped coming. Jean offered the same business deal that had initiated her start in the juice bar business; she offered to sell the business to a girl who worked for her at the juice bar for the price of the inventory. The young girl paid $400, and Jean left the juice bar. Two months later the spa closed.

Another chapter in Jean's life came to a close, but as she had learned previously, when God closed one opportunity, He was preparing a new one! Jean was eager to follow after His leading!

CHAPTER 3

MY MISSIONARY

In 1981, Jean started regularly attending North Way Christian Community in Wexford. Through her intimate conversations with God, she had developed recognition of His Voice. Often she would share something God had spoken to her. It was not something she heard through an audible voice but something she received in her thoughts – within her spirit. To her, it was a perfectly natural form of communication.

We were in a meeting one time. There was a woman sitting next to me, and I'd never met her before. I said to her, "You don't have to beg. God knows your need, and He's going to send you whatever you need to go." Well, she was missionary, and I didn't know that. I had no idea that was what it was.

Mark Geppert was the Director of Missions at North Way at that time, and he became acquainted with Jean's passion for God. In 1987 he announced to her, "Jean, you need to go to Scotland…there is a fishing village over there that needs you." [Inverollachy and Cairnbulg, Scotland – two small villages that merged into one community]

The women of this village had no pastor to minister to them because the pastor would not come to the women's homes. The men went to sea on Sunday evening after church service and did not return until Saturday evening. It was not appropriate or acceptable for the minister to go into a woman's home without her husband's presence, so these women were "sheep without a shepherd." By this time, Jean had long accepted her call from God; however, she had not extended her ministry beyond the confines of her own country. Was God indeed calling her to be the missionary that her *comare* had proclaimed at her birth?

In faith, Jean purchased her ticket to Scotland, and with $300 in her pocket, she arrived at JFK Airport with a female traveling companion ready to embark on this new adventure. The attendant at the desk asked where she was traveling to and Jean responded that they were going to Scotland. The woman replied, "Not with this passport; it's expired!" In complete disbelief, Jean examined the document – the passport had expired the previous year! The attendant proposed that Jean and her friend stay in New York for the weekend and go to the American Embassy on the following Monday to secure a valid passport. When Jean asked what that would cost, the woman replied that it would be about $500 – Jean had only $300 for her entire trip. Jean began to fervently pray.

I said, "I've got to be in Scotland." She said, "Is it an emergency?" I said, "Yes, I'm supposed to be speaking on Sunday morning." The woman rolled her eyes – an emergency was supposed to be of life or death importance – speaking at a fishing village didn't qualify for that! She gave me a number to call in Washington, D.C. and said, "Maybe they can give you a temporary passport." I called the number and a young man answered. I said, "My name is Jean Yanakos, and I have an invalid passport. It's an emergency – I have to get to Scotland." He said, "Stay right where you are, and I'll call you right back. I'll have someone who'll be able to help you."

Another woman at the desk said, "This will never happen. You will never get a passport." So I said to my companion, "Call Pittsburgh and ask everyone you know to pray." When I got the operator, she said, "Who is at your home that can let you make a collect call?" Obviously, there was no one at home; I was there! She said, "Is there another phone?"

Jean gave her the phone number for a family member. The number was called – then it disconnected! Three times the call disconnected; Jean was getting frantic – the plane was scheduled to leave in 15 minutes. Finally, the family member accepted the collect call. That didn't resolve anything, but it did allow the process to continue.

Meanwhile, their luggage was taken off the plane and their seats were assigned to other passengers since departure was so imminent. When the collect call finally went through, the woman from Washington, D.C. began her inquiry with Jean.

"Didn't you know your passport was not valid?" Jean's inner voice wanted to scream, "Yes, of course I knew, but I like going through all this mess! " Miraculously, Jean held her tongue!

"No, I had no idea. I thought it was all right."

"We never do this," the woman stated formally. Jean said nothing and remained on the line. The woman repeated her statement as if repetition would allow the reality of her statement to sink in.

"Did you hear me? We never do this!" she firmly repeated. She continued her inquiry, asking if a death was the reason for the urgency of the trip.

"No, it's just that I'm a special speaker, and I'm supposed to speak on Sunday. They're bringing me in from the States."

Again, she announced, "We don't do this!" Within the next few minutes of conversation, she repeated how impossible it was to grant this exception at least a dozen times. Jean persisted – she did not give up; she did not give in. Finally, the Washington authority ordered Jean to put the woman at the desk back on the line.

A smug smirk crossed the face of the attendant, but it was quickly replaced with wide-eyed astonishment as the attendant began to write down the orders of the D.C. woman. When she finished writing, she returned the phone to Jean. The Washington woman formally declared the verdict.

"This is a temporary passport I'm giving you. When you get to Scotland, you have to go to Edinburg and get a real passport at the cost of $80."

"That's fine! That's fine!" Jean replied.

The temporary passport was granted; the luggage was secured and quickly loaded on the plane. Jean and her companion were assigned new seats. Each time they passed through customs or security checks, Jean's friend was detained and searched despite her valid passport, while Jean with her scribbled temporary passport was never questioned. Once seated on the plane Jean berated herself and complained to God about her own inadequacies.

How could I get on a plane with no passport? That's not even common sense. Even with faith I should have a little common sense. I said, "Lord, I feel stupid and so dumb that I had not taken care of that passport. I looked at it six months before and it never registered that it was expired!" But the Lord spoke to me and said, "Anybody can go to Scotland with a valid passport. [Isn't that the truth!?!] But to get to Scotland without one – that was a miracle!" When we were on the plane, we had lost the good seats we were supposed to have; we were separated. Still when I sat down in my seat, I breathed such a heavy sigh of relief. All I could think about was that He covers us under the shadow of His wings. There I was riding on His wings.

The departure from JFK was a sharp contrast to the 8' x 10' waiting room upon arrival at the Scottish airport. It was the size of Jean's kitchen! She and her companion scanned the tiny facility for the receiving party. They had been informed that a tall, 6 foot 4 inch bearded gentleman would meet them at the terminal. Instead, they saw two women cowering in a corner. Jean approached them and learned that they were the assigned greeters. The women offered to take Jean and her friend to a tearoom for refreshments after the long transatlantic flight.

Prior to the tearoom, Jean asked a stop at the bank to exchange $100 of her American money into pounds. Jean stuffed the pounds into her sweater pocket. After enjoying the delicious pastries and teas and then perusing several local shops, Jean and her party retreated to the home of her hostess. Melting into a wonderful bed with 8 inches of soft down was a welcome relief after the challenges of their travels.

In the morning, Jean felt refreshed and started to count her money for the transactions of the day. The $100 exchanged into pounds was missing! She informed her hostess and together, they counted again and again. It was gone! Jean recalled that she had wiped her nose several times the previous day and stuffed the Kleenex into her pocket. The pounds must have become entangled with the tissue and fallen out! Her hostess assured her that it was not a problem and called various stores they had visited – to no avail. Finally, her hostess contacted the police station.

The policeman said someone found $100. "What denominations did you have?" they asked. I said it was $100 in American money, but I didn't know what denominations that would be in pounds. He said, "Well, we will keep the returned money here for three days. After three days, you can come up and have it if no one claims it."

I thought this is great faith. Can you imagine in America if someone found $100 and they took it to the police station? Then the police would actually hold it and say, "Oh yeah, we have your money, and we'll hold for it three days." We went back three days later, and I got my hundred dollars. It was just one miracle after another the whole time.

The pastor had provided names and addresses of women who were "shut-ins". He expected that Jean and her companion would make visitations. Inspired by what God had already done thus far in her travels, Jean was not content to sit around. After three days, the pastor had not yet come to see the women to confirm their duties. Jean grew restless; she was eager to usher in the Presence of God.

"I don't think the Lord brought us thousands of miles just to have fellowship with you – although I am enjoying your fel-

lowship," I shared with our hostess. "We have come in the ministry of Elijah and Elisha, and we are going to pray."

We were reading the 17th chapter of John and at the end, I began to pray. As I did, I felt something happen to my throat that I've never had since. I felt like I was sucking on lemons. I began to speak. I knew what I was saying in my mind, but as it was coming out of my mouth I didn't recognize what it was. To this day it seems creepy. I later found out that the message that I was speaking, my hostess said, was the perfect "Belger" tongue. My hostess, Chris Patterson, wept and wept and told me what I had said.

Then the power of God fell, and she started to prophecy over me [the hostess], but the awesome uncanny thing was that she prophesied in our exact dialect. I don't believe anyone could ever, or at least very few people would, manage to speak this dialect on their own. It was perfect "Belger" as we would say. People have lived 40 – 50 years who have been in commons in the village, and they cannot speak it properly. So it's only by the miraculous power of the Holy Spirit and what was spoken was: "I am speaking in your tongue so that you could never doubt your calling in God the rest of your life." It must have been exactly what happened on the day of Pentecost. Hallelujah - our God reigns! [Excerpt from Chris Patterson's letter –7/10/87]

For three weeks, Jean ministered to these Scottish women. Every day she led them in a Bible study, sharing the rich nuggets of truth that she had learned from her intimate study and prayer time with the Lord. Jean expounded on the Word of God, explaining that the miracles and wonders of God's power were available now, just as they were long ago. She modeled effective prayers and encouraged them to trust God the Father to teach them and lead them into deeper spiritual waters. Day after day, the women experienced God faithfully responding to their hungry cries.

One of the villagers was unable to accompany his fellow fishermen due to an injury, and he warily observed the prayer-filled adventures of the women. From the safe distance of the kitchen, he overheard and witnessed heavenly antics that were beyond his worldly experience. This American woman was stirring up supernatural powers, and he stated in his Scottish brogue, "She scares the hell outa me!" If only he had realized that was precisely what she wanted to do!

The families of the small fishing village were deeply touched by the examples and prayers of Jean and her traveling companion. They received the two women as gifts from God and recognized that the lives of these families were forever transformed by these two precious women.

There is a remnant of people in our Church who will never forget the ministry of these two prophets of God. There must be about a dozen families...whose lives have never been the same again. They have been revolutionized by the power of God, and the work the Holy Spirit has done and is doing is awesome and fearsome in our midst. [Excerpt from Chris Patterson's letter –7/10/87]

The day before their scheduled departure, Jean led the daily Bible study then, as usual, asked if there were any special needs for prayer. A sweet grandmother named Irene approached Jean and put a six-month old baby upon Jean's lap. When Jean inquired of the woman what she wanted prayer for, Irene responded in a thick Scottish brogue, "Would you pray for William?" The loving grandmother then exposed baby William's hands. The knuckles had only nubs; there were no fingers. Jean was stunned.

I looked at that and I thought, "Oh, Lord, what are you doing to me? This is the most impossible thing - to pray for someone who has no fingers! Oh, come on! Can't You give me somebody who has a headache? Why would You give me a young boy who has no fingers?"

I knew I was leaving the next day and I thought, "Okay, I'm going to pray." My heart was going boom, boom, boom… because I didn't want to look like an idiot! I knew those fingers weren't going to grow out right then. So I said a simple prayer, "Lord, heal the baby's hands and let the fingers grow." That was it! It didn't really matter if the baby got healed or not – I wasn't going to be there. They can't blame me if nothing happens." I left the next day, and I was saying, "Thank God, I'm going home."

Fifteen years later, Jean returned to Scotland. She visited the same quaint village and went with the congregation to the North Sea to participate in a service of salvation and baptism. Jean wore two pairs of long johns, a pair of coveralls, a cape and a coat. She could barely walk with the cumbersome layers of clothing she wore. Despite her fear of water and being unable to swim, she participated in the baptism, and even lost a shoe in the process! At the close of the service, the villagers wrapped her in blankets as she stood on the pebbled beach. She was shivering from the intense cold, but what happened next more than warmed Jean's heart!

I heard someone calling my name. There's this woman running down the beach and she's dragging a teenager behind her. She kept screaming my name, "Oh, Sister Jean! Sister Jean!" I remembered her, and Irene said, "Do you remember William? This is the baby that you prayed for!" And I said, "Really?" She said to the young boy, "Take your hand out!" She grabbed his hand and pushed it right in my face - and every finger had grown back!

Excitedly Irene invited Jean to their home that evening to hear William, an accomplished musician, play the keyboard, flute and drums. For two hours, he confirmed the divine healing with masterful music; awards from various competitions were displayed throughout the home, further confirming the young man's musical talents.

I was never so shocked in my whole life! To see this baby that I have prayed for – this baby who had nothing! If you made a fist, all you would see were the bumps on his knuckles

– no fingers there whatsoever! I said to her, "When did this happen?" "Within a week of when you prayed - first one knob came out and it began to grow. That's how we get teeth, you know – one at a time. The last one to grow was his thumb. They had to operate on it a couple times because it wasn't the way it needed to be for working." When I looked and saw what God had done, I was amazed!

Jean was stunned by the awesome display of God's divine healing, and her faith was radically bolstered. She realized God did heal, God did answer prayer – not because the prayer was articulate or deserved a divine response, but because God desired to heal His people. And despite her personal doubt regarding His Divine Purpose, He allowed her to participate in His Plan!

In her humanness, Jean did have a few words of complaint to deliver to Mark Geppert, the Missionary Director at North Way who commissioned her on this whole adventure. Things had not been exactly as he had said they would be. She and her friend were not met at the airport by the tall man as promised, the pastor had not been available to initiate their time of instructing the women, she and her companion had to step out in faith to get things started.

I kind of complained to Mark about it and he said "Well, you had the Holy Ghost, didn't you? That's all you need!" So that settled that. I could've shot him at the time.

The new chapter in her life was clearly launched. Jean began to travel to different countries in response to teaching engagements, often traveling with her daughter Carol. God continued to open doors of opportunity, and Jean walked through them.

Jean and Carol attended a ladies' retreat in Singapore. About 275 women were in attendance and were staying at the hotel with four women to a room. An English woman who was an officer in the Women's Aglow Association was at the retreat. She was close to 6 feet tall and stately; in contrast, the Chinese women were very small in stature and petite. The women walked down the aisle into the conference room to take their seats for the meeting. At meetings like this, God would often give Jean's "words" of revelation that had a startling impact for the recipient.

The English woman was coming down the aisle to find a seat. I said to her, "I heard what you said this morning in your room." And she said, "What?" I said, "You said to the Lord, 'Why have you made me so and allowed me to come to a country where I am out of place all the time? I'm too big for the women. I'm too tall, and my speech confuses them because of my accent. Why did you make me the way that I am?'" When I told her that, she started to cry. I said, "That isn't to embarrass you. That's to let you know that God loves you, and He knows the concerns that you have." Then I quoted Psalm 139 to her. I said, "It is no accident! God has placed you so that you are head and shoulders over everybody else. That is a good place to be!"

The next day the same woman walked into the meeting room. Again Jean spoke aloud what the English woman had said in the morning in her room. The woman was stunned.

And she said, "Is there anything that the Lord doesn't hear?" And I said, "Well, that's true of all of us. He knows every word – He knows every thought before we even say it!" That is even worse to me – that He knows my thoughts before I speak them. That's why I've always tried to be an encourager and an exhorter – to build people up and not to cut them down.

We [the English woman and Jean] became fast friends, because I said, "You can't keep criticizing how God made you because He loved you enough to make you exactly who you are and He gave you the parents you have – He knew that you were going to be a tall woman. He knew you were going to be a very stately woman." That kind of settled her down. She recognized that this was of God. Then she had to go back to England.

Jean experienced both supernatural and practical lessons in China. She met a wealthy woman whose husband was a banker; he had cancer. Regrettably, the couple had experienced much financial abuse at the hands of Christian speakers. The speakers sought out the couple – perhaps because of their wealth – and delivered distorted teachings and prophecies. They told the woman that she should dispose of her elaborate set of Wedgewood china because the pattern had an elephant on it – the elephant was "of the devil". In desperate obedience she got rid of the dishes; she broke all 15 place settings. They also prayed over her husband and prophesied that her husband would be healed. Their two sons were shocked by the abuse, and they rejected Christianity. They would not have anything to do with God because of this abuse. When Jean arrived in China, the two sons had become atheists.

When I met her she said to me, "I don't believe in prophecy." I said, "I'm not going to prophesy over you or your husband." I learned some of the abuses that went on in the name of Christianity. As Christians, we have to be careful. Like the Bible says, "Let your 'yeah' be 'yeah' and your 'nay' be 'nay'." It better be that way, especially when it comes to things about money.

She would tell me this one needed money for a building, and that one needed money for a school – so she and her husband gave $100,000 dollars to this one and $300,000 to that one – why? – because they were trying to buy a healing. "You give and God will give back to you" was what they were told. I made up my mind that I was not going to get next to this woman. I didn't want her to think that I was going to be next to her because of her money.

Then her husband died, and she became bitter against God and bitter against anybody that was a speaker or preacher. She never trusted anything that I said. I tried to get a relationship going. It ended up that she did become my friend. She asked me to pray for her, but there was no change. She loved God as much a she could and as much as she was able, but she would remember the abuses of other Christians. I kept saying, "That was then and this is now. I never asked you for a dime and I didn't expect anything from you!" That was why our relationship grew.

Jean was mindful of the awesome responsibility she carried; she came in the name of the Lord. As a Christian, she was the visible representative of Christ, and she knew that her actions would impact the reception that others would give to Him. As a redeemed sinner, she did not carry His image perfectly, but her goal was to become more and more like Him in her daily conduct.

In addition to the practical application of representing the Lord, Jean continued to be a humble servant amazed by God's faithfulness as He used her in "teaching, preaching, and healing" wherever she traveled.

I went to China. I went to Russia. I went to England. I went to Germany. I went to Puerto Rico. I went to Malaysia. I went to Singapore. I went to Morocco. I saw great miracles that happened. It was just one miracle after another the whole time.

I knew there was nothing in me. There was no good thing in me. I would be walking the floor or I would be walking outside and I would say to the Lord, "Lord, if You don't show up, nothing will happen." I guess the Lord got kind of tired of hearing me fussing and complaining like that, and I heard Him say, "Alright already, I told you I will never leave you or forsake you!" And He never did!

She knew, all too well, that the supernatural power manifested in response to her prayers was not of her – it was of Him, the One who so faithfully taught her of His heart and will. What a wonder to be used of Him – what a wonder to be His Missionary!

CHAPTER 4

THE DARLING OF MY HEART

A unique bond exists between a mother and daughter, and the relationship between Jean and her daughter Carol attests to that. From her early years, Carol was stubborn and confrontational, and frequently there was a power struggle between these two strong-willed females. In addition to the predictable conflicts of a developing daughter, the home atmosphere was filled with the uncertainties of living with an alcoholic father. Jean did her best to protect her children from the irrational wrath and abuse.

While under the influence, Jean's husband would succumb to rants and rages, and he frequently threw Jean and her two children out of the house, irrespective of weather conditions. Often clothed in nightgowns and pajamas without footwear, the threesome would hover together while Jean contacted her sister and brother-in-law, who came to the rescue and gave the evicted trio a haven in their home. Life was tenuous; nonetheless, Jean clung to her faith in God and dragged her children with her, willing or not, to receive teachings about God and to experience His Presence.

More out of rebellion than love, Carol married at the age of 21. She ran off with a guy, who was far below the standard her mother desired for her, on the last day of college. The marriage was a miserable one, filled with abuse and unfaithfulness, and the relationship ended after 2 short years. In 1970, Carol met Sam, a school teacher who worked in the room next to hers. They fell in love and started planning their marriage. Jean was delighted because Sam was a "wonderful guy." Carol had found the love of her life, and she beamed with delight. At the rehearsal dinner, Carol graciously introduced the wedding party to one another, but as she did, Jean heard a word from God that disrupted her supportive joy.

Carol introduced me to Rick and said, "This is Rick, Sam's best man." I said, "Hi!" While I said that, in my mind and in my heart I hear the words, "This is her husband." I could have died because she was getting married to Sam the very next morning! I thought, "Oh, God, I don't dare tell her that!" I didn't know what to think!

I thought, "Maybe that's the devil just trying to scare me." I have a habit when things come to me and I don't understand them and I don't have clarity, I put them on my back burner. If you ever hear my teachings, you know there's always a back burner that you can put everything on - eventually it will come to pass. I never said a word to her.

The wedding went on as planned.

Eighteen months later, Carol was 27 years old and happily married. Her husband drove her in from Johnstown, Pennsylvania for a family gathering, and after the event, they stayed at Jean's home until it was time for them to leave. Being the typical Italian mother, Jean coaxed them to stay for dinner and made her son-in-law's favorite dish, Italian spaghetti. In due time, stomachs were full, dishes were cleared, and the satiated couple left for home about seven o'clock in the evening.

At 10:30PM that same night, Jean's husband received a call from a hospital in Greensburg, Pennsylvania, a town close to Johnstown, brutally stating that if they wanted to see their daughter alive, they had to get to the hospital in less than half an hour. Carol's husband was already dead, and she was almost dead.

On the way to the hospital, God's grace and love were prevalent - so prevalent that I was numb to everything and everyone around me. I kept hearing the words, 'It's all right. I am in control.'

Then, I heard the Lord ask me the same question as when she was seven years old: "Are you willing to give me the darling of your heart?" I then spoke to the Lord in my heart and said the same thing I had said 21 years ago: "If You want her, You can have her, but You've got to give me Your grace to go through this." I began to reason with the Lord, and in my heart I knew I had been given 21 years of having my daughter and a peace came over me.

I didn't know what we would see when we went to the hospital. I didn't know what to expect, except her husband of only eighteen months was killed instantly. When they allowed us to enter into the intensive care unit, what I saw sent me into shock!

Carol's injuries were extensive. Her head was wrapped in bandages due to an open skull fracture; her face looked like it had been chopped with a meat cleaver. There were major lacerations on the left side of her face, and her left eye protruded from the eye socket onto her cheekbone. Carol's front teeth on the top and bottom had been knocked out or broken off. A massive laceration from her lip to underneath her chin was stitched with thick, black thread. In addition to her facial injuries, Carol's spine was broken in three places, her pelvis was shattered, and her hip was fractured in multiple places. There were severe injuries to her internal organs; her uterus was lacerated causing a spontaneous abortion of the child she did not know she had conceived.

The doctor said if she lived for the next 72 hours, she might survive, but her mental capacities would be severely limited. For two days, the family maintained a vigilant watch at the hospital; they dare not leave while Carol's life remained in a precarious balance. On the third day, a gracious Christian woman whose son was in the same intensive care room offered her home for respite, and Jean's family convinced her to accept the kindness and get some sleep.

I went to bed at 11 o'clock that night. Around three o'clock in the morning of the third day, I was awakened with these words, "Carol has passed the crisis, and she will live and glorify Me in her body."

I rose and went to the hospital where family members were taking turns going in for 5 minutes every hour. I came running down the hall almost shouting, "Carol has passed the crisis and she will live!" At that time, my husband was not a true believer and asked me, "Are you sure?" and I said, "Yes! Yes!"

At one point early in the recovery, Carol awakened from her coma and sat straight up in bed. She cried out her husband's name and strained to reach out and touch him, for she saw him at the end of her bed. She desperately tried to bring him to her. Later when Carol finally came out of the coma, she remembered that experience and relayed that she was on the other side in Heaven with Sam. She'd chosen to stay there, but her husband convinced her that she must return to earth.

Carol was in and out of a coma for the next month, and Jean was steadfastly by her side. Jean refused to return to Pittsburgh that whole time. She stayed in the same clothes and hand washed her personal effects every night. She was a mother on a mission – overseeing the word God had given her and stubbornly holding fast to that promise.

The whole time that Carol lay in a coma, the Lord spoke to me that I was to send her healing love. I had no clue what that meant. I was given instructions that I was to tell her over and over how much God loved her, how much I loved her, how much her father loved her, and how much her brother loved her – even though she was unconscious. Most of the time we were telling her how much God loved her and was with her. That's all she heard for one solid month - how much the Father loved her. I am convinced that brought about the recovery more than anything else. Healing love is what the world needs. The Father's love needs to be revealed in these days more than any other revelation. It's healing love.

The family remained steadfast in their diligent presence, care, devotion, and expressions of love. It was a testimony to all who observed them in the hospital that, in the midst of such a life-threatening crisis, this family demonstrated "such love".

Throughout the initial 30 days of recuperation, Carol's broken hip had not been diagnosed. With attention to all of the other life-threatening injuries, it was somehow overlooked. Carol was transported to Pittsburgh by ambulance for treatment. When they tried to operate, the procedure was impeded by the length of time that had elapsed – the bone had grown in the 30 day period; corrective pins could not be inserted.

The overall prognosis was grim: Carol's one leg would be 2 inches shorter than the other and she would walk with a limp; she would have brain damage from the severe concussion; her left eye was extensively damaged, she would never see out of it, and it would be removed. That surgery was delayed only because of the neurosurgeon's concern that the anesthetics would cause further damage to her fragile brain.

In one month, I had been told she would not live, but if she did live, she would be a vegetable and never walk right again and never be able to see and her eye would have to be removed. But the Lord had said, "She will glorify God in her body."

The recovery was painstakingly slow. For two years, Carol stayed in a hospital bed in Jean's living room. With Jean's faith-filled and sometimes stubborn oversight, Carol began the rehabilitation of learning how to walk and regaining normal daily functioning. As her facial scars healed, other cosmetic conditions needed to be addressed – what could be done with her teeth? Through the accident, Carol had lost much of the supportive bone in her mouth. If false teeth were constructed, there was no bone to hold them in her mouth. Step by step, step by step… and throughout the arduous process, prayers were offered for her practically all over the world.

About six months after the operation, I was kneeling and praying for a specific family need. As I was praying, I saw a message come across my mind like a tickertape message that assured me the answer would come on Wednesday. The strange thing was that another message was appearing right underneath that one, and it was almost out of sight. Before it was totally out of sight, I read it and it said that Carol my daughter would receive 90 to 95% of her sight. I said, "Lord, I'll take that, too!"

The first prayer was answered the following Wednesday. I knew if that part of the message was true, my daughter's would come true also.

There were numerous consultations with eye specialists. First of all, most expressed utter amazement that Carol even had an eye and that it had not shriveled. Secondly, they were amazed that she had any sight at all. The pupils in both her eyes are fixed open and injured; one eye had no iris. She received multiple surgeries with specialists all over the United States due to the complexities of the injuries.

Through constant prayer, the Grace of God, and the miracle of medicine, Carol's vision had been preserved. Because there was a significant discrepancy in the visual acuity of each of her eyes, she was unable to use corrective lens. Her brain would not be able to reconcile the drastic difference between the two eyes. However, if she would lose sight in the right eye, she could receive corrective surgery and magnification for the injured eye for sight.

Five years into her recovery, Carol disclosed to Jean a secret injury that had been as devastating as the injuries from the car accident. She recalled the evictions of Jean and her children by her alcoholic father and the refuge that Jean sought for them with her sister and brother-in-law. Carol confessed that the brother-in-law, her uncle, molested her from the time she was 4 years of age until 8 years of age. Jean was stunned! How could that be??? As the mother, she had sought refuge for her family and instead she had ushered them into the throes of abuse!

Of course, I almost died. I went through a horrible guilt. How did I not recognize the redness and bruises on her vagina? How stupid was I? Why didn't the doctors tell me? [Jean had doctored with Carol for a "vaginal infection" for several years, and Carol had a D & C at age 8 which seemed to clear up the "infection"]. On and on I played the tape recorder in my mind. There came a time of confrontation with my sister and her husband, and of course, they denied it for 10 years. They did not speak to me. In my heart, I hated this man for how he abused my child. I simply could not and would not forgive him.

Nonetheless, Carol's healing continued – healing of body and healing of soul. In the midst of the seemingly interminable process, God delivered a precious gift! While Carol was recuperating in Jean's living room, Rick, Sam's best man, began finishing the house that Sam had begun building for his wife. Using his own materials and working in addition to his own occupation, he labored from roof to basement – a labor of love.

Carol remained a widow for seven years, experiencing the reviving of her body and soul as she slowly healed. She then concluded that she needed to learn to live again and said she was ready to start dating. Rick announced, "If you're going to start dating, I want to be the first one in line." Allowing her heart to surrender to love again was not an easy process and Carol wrestled with her own thoughts and feelings. In the end, Rick's tenderhearted care and faithful service won her over.

She said, "He's too good to lose," and that was what settled it. They ran off and got married, but they have the best marriage that I've seen anywhere – barring none! They have a very, very good marriage. And they love each other equally. I mean it's not just one-sided – she loves him as much as he loves her. It's precious!

In addition to delivering a loving life partner, God also delivered a prognosis drastically different from the one the doctors had originally proclaimed. They said if she lived, Carol would be a vegetable; she finished her doctorate in cognitive therapy with a specialization in child molestation. They said she would walk with a limp; she does not walk with a limp because there is no difference in the length of her legs. They said her eye would be removed; the eye remained. Although she has not yet received 90-95% of her vision, only God knows the medical advancements in surgery and magnification that will come. Carol has had numerous plastic surgeries for her chin and eyes, and yes, the dilemma with the dentures was resolved, so that her outward appearance is refreshingly beautiful!

Praise God, she is a beautiful woman of God physically and spiritually. Such compassion she has for those that are troubled emotionally and physically! Now we know that all the pain this child has suffered has not been in vain. In II Corinthians 13:45 we understand that God the Father gives us comfort in our trials, so we can comfort others who are going through what we have gone through. This was not only a test for me as a mother, but for the whole family and for my daughter personally.

Carol gratefully acknowledges the rich heritage she has received from her mother's words, teachings, and life example. As a Mother's Day tribute, Carol penned the following:

HAPPY MOTHER'S DAY

Life Lessons Modeled by My Mother

- The Faithfulness of God
- Trust in God
- Pray and Read the Bible
- Never Give Up
- Believe in the Future
- Hope
- You Can Always Achieve If You Work For It
- Work for What You Want
- How to Dress Well 😊
- The Love of Adventure and Travel
- Believe In Myself
- I Can Do All Things Through Christ
- The Value of Never Quitting
- Perseverance
- Never Let Your Gender Stop You

But most importantly
THAT MY MOTHER LOVES ME!!!!

Thanks for Everything.   I Love You
Carol

Preparing for the Tent Ministry

Setting up for the Tent Meeting

Serving at the Juice Bar

Staying with a Scottish Hostess

Boarding a Scottish "Taxi"

Baptizing in the North Sea

Ministering in Singapore

Meeting with a Singapore Hostess

Chatting with the Aglow Englishwoman

Distributing Bibles in Russia

Visiting a Russian Prison

Meeting Locals in Morraco with Carol

Dining in a Morracan Restaurant

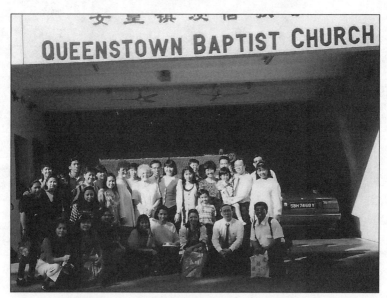

Gathering Together in Queenstown

Leading Worship in Singapore

Rejoicing with Charlie and Sharon

Riding a Camel with Carol

Feeding a "Jumping" Congregation

Sightseeing in Italy

Praising God at a Women's Retreat

Celebrating her 75th Birthday

CHAPTER 5

REVELATIONS FROM GOD

Jean did not have the funds or the time to attend seminary, so she spent endless hours reading the Bible and praying that God would reveal Himself to her. She had an insatiable appetite for the Scriptures and never tired of listening to hear what the Lord would teach her.

In addition to her own personal study, God provided three significant mentors who expanded Jean's spiritual understanding. One of those mentors was her husband's sister, Elaine, a very devout Christian.

My sister-in-law, Elaine, was very, very kind. She was in a hard way as far as her marriage. It wasn't a perfect marriage. Well, there are very few perfect marriages. Anyway, she would go out of her way to encourage me. All the time, she played the piano – oh, she played the piano and the organ, and she sang with me! She never took a lesson - the Holy Spirit taught her how to play. I have a pretty good voice and I can sing well if people play in my key, but in any church that I've ever been, no one plays in my key. She could look at a song, see the notes and transpose it into my key – which is almost impossible – at least to me!

We would sit for hours and she would teach me all the hymns, night after night after night. We would just sit and sing and sing. That's how I really learned to praise God because she played all these old songs; we would go over them and she would teach me them. It was amazing!

She became my organist when I was a pastor. We never had a set list of what to sing and how long it would take like they do today. We never did any of that! We just started to sing, and if we sang one song for 20 minutes, that was okay! There were so many times when I would open my mouth to sing and she would already have the first note of what I was singing – we were so in tune together. We just loved to worship!

Elaine was a diabetic and she became very ill. She died at the age of 62. She had experienced much pain in her own life, but she was always there to encourage Jean.

She always built me up because she had gone through the same thing. That is what I especially teach women. What you're going through right now, you're going through it not only for yourself! What you are going through is for someone else, too! One day God is going to send a person to you that needs to hear that same experience.

So Elaine was always a blessing to me because of what I saw in her life. She taught me how to hold on, to believe God, and how to praise. I learned a lot from watching how she handled the trials that she was going through. She was just a very lovely person with a fervent love of God.

Another mentor was Jean's Baptist neighbor, Mrs. Alexander, who lived in the adjacent house; she called her home *the House of the Lord.* She would say, "Whatever you need is in this house. If you don't have it, it's in this house!" Each Saturday night Mrs. Alexander called Jean to ask if Jean had something to wear for church the following day. If Jean lacked attire, Mrs. Alexander found something appropriate in *the House of the Lord.* Mrs. Alexander also demonstrated her faith in practical acts of kindness. Every Thursday she went to the local hospital and distributed flowers she had picked, as well as an apple and an orange, to every person in the hospital. For four years Jean accompanied her on these missions of mercy. Mrs. Alexander also made chicken soup from the chickens her husband raised.

This woman walked up the street every day of her life with two shopping bags full of chicken soup that she made. Her husband would raise chickens and then he killed them; then she would make chicken soup. She'd use one chicken for about 30 or 40 quarts of chicken soup. I would say to her, "Mrs. Alexander, there's nothing left on those bones!" She would say, "Oh, yes! We can use that for another batch." She would take all the bones out of that kettle and make another batch of soup. I would say, "That can't taste like chicken soup!" She would say, "Oh, yes, it does!" I learned then how God provided. This woman had such faith, and she had such a love for people – always wanting to do and give.

Jean's mother-in-law tried to witness to Mrs. Alexander about the Holy Spirit and speaking in tongues. Mrs. Alexander always refrained from speaking ill about Jean's mother-in-law, but she did clarify to Jean her strong opinion about this doctrinal belief.

She would say, "You know there's nothing wrong with them speaking in tongues, but if you don't have love, you don't have anything!" I learned from her! I learned how to memorize the Scriptures because she taught me. She was really a wonderful mentor on love and the goodness of God and the faithfulness of God. And she never doubted that her husband would get saved and delivered. They moved down to South Carolina; he got saved and became a deacon in the church. She came back and she said, "I told you! With God all things are possible!"

Hannah Bernard was another woman who had an enriching influence on Jean's life. Hannah and Jean met at a retreat in New Hampshire in which Hannah was the morning speaker, and Jean was the evening speaker. The two women developed a deep mutual respect for one another and Hannah was Jean's mentor for 15 years.

She had the most wonderful lessons of anyone I ever heard in my life. She would say to me how much God loved me and talk of the joy of the Lord. We had rooms next to each other, and I would hear her laughing and laughing and laughing. She would be laughing so loudly that I would put my ear up against the wall because the walls were paper thin. I would think, "What is she doing over there?" While I was listening she would say, "Why, of course, Lord! Why didn't I think of that?" She'd just heard something from the Lord.

Jean and Hannah could not have been more opposite! Jean was Pentecostal with a tambourine and all the accompanying noise; Hannah was high Anglican and very reserved in her expressions. During the retreat meetings, Hannah sat in the first seat of the front row with her hands folded and her feet firmly planted side by side on the floor.

We'd all be clapping and everyone singing, but she was sitting there prim and proper. After the meeting was over, she'd come up to me and tell me one thing that she got out of the service. She came up to me and said, "Oh, Darling, you blessed my soul!" I knew she was only doing that to make me feel good.

Hannah was a missionary in Israel for 43 years. She knew many languages and she was proficient in Hebrew. She had extensive knowledge of the language and knew that each Hebrew word had two meanings. Her teaching on the Beatitudes offered a prescription for divine health; the Beatitudes speak clearly of the various parts of the body.

I learned about the physical body through her teachings. She was just a wonderful, wonderful person. She was a vegetarian and then she became a fruitetarian. She wouldn't kill anything to eat. What happened was she had a rabbit for a pet; her mother cooked the rabbit for Easter. When Hannah found out it was her pet that was served for Easter dinner, she vowed that she would never eat another piece of meat just to satisfy her flesh. She lived to be 95 years of age, and she wrote about 46 manuscripts. She was one of the greatest teachers I ever had! She poured into my life and she was really wonderful!

From these three women, Jean gleaned diverse aspects of God's character, and she gained a deep appreciation of the truths that can be gained from different members of the Body of Christ. This knowledge opened Jean's receptiveness to God's wisdom and knowledge from varied sources throughout her life.

Jean loved learning of God and loved communing with Him. She learned to hear His voice – not an audible expression, but that deep inner whispering that was distinctively different from her own voice. Often while she was soaking in the bathtub she would hear that Voice or He would awaken her in the middle of the night. Sometimes His revelations would come in the form of dreams or visions. Jean was mindful to ponder the things that she learned and write them down.

Sometimes she needed to continue to pray and ask the Lord for clarification to decipher the meaning of her revelations, but Jean delighted in hearing from God. Recently a long-lost journal was unearthed in her papers; the writings were penned more than 15 years ago! Jean treasured reviewing the visions and revelations, amazed that they held the same refreshing life that she had experienced when she first received them.

I had a vision that has remained with me all these years. First in the vision, I found myself on the edge of the sea. I was fishing with a rod and was catching one fish at a time. A thought entered my mind, "Why not get a boat and get further out in the ocean to catch more fish with a net?" That I did, and it was going quite well. I was catching 6, 7, even 8 fish at a time. As I was on the ocean, I saw a school of fish in the middle of the ocean. The thought occurred to me that it would be more expedient to get a whole school of fish rather than the way I had been fishing. Somehow I managed to capture a school of fish in my net. It filled my boat to overflowing and my boat sank to the bottom of the ocean floor.

All of a sudden I saw on the floor of the ocean a beautiful object. I could not make out what it was, but I knew it was very precious and I had to have it! I donned a diver suit and with weighted shoes proceeded to get out of the boat to retrieve the jewel. It was multicolored and beautifully radiant. I was spellbound as I watched it.

It kept moving at a slow pace. I had to walk very carefully because I didn't want to stir up the silt. That would make the water muddy and obscure the jewel. As I kept my eyes on the jewel, it started to burrow into a sand dune and I knew it was about to disappear. So I made a lunge and grabbed it with both hands, grappling it before it went too far into the dune.

The moment I had it into my hands, I suddenly I felt an overwhelming power grab me by the feet and it lifted me up until I was on top of the water. As I reached the top of the water, I raised this beautiful jewel over my head. The sun shone on it, and it sent beautiful rays to every part of the shores of the ocean. As I held this jewel over my head, people began to come from every tribe, people, and nation to see the light. I thought of the Scripture John 12:32, "And I, when I am lifted up from the earth, will draw all people to myself."" That was the end of the vision.

Jean delighted in her personal parable, and discerned the importance of drawing all into the family of God, whether one-on-one or varying sized groups. She also recognized that a relationship with Christ was a priceless jewel. For that reason, Jesus was to be lifted up – sharing His glory with no other.

As Jean continued to grow in her knowledge and understanding of God's ways, she desired that her life would reflect His Glory. That prompted her to pray that God would give her grace to forgive her sister and brother-in-law, specifically for the unspeakable, heinous acts of molestation that her brother-in-law had committed. As a mother, it was unforgivable, yet she knew that forgiveness was something God proclaimed and specified, particularly in the Lord's Prayer. Her soul longed for justice, yet her heart's desire was to please God and walk in a way that would glorify Him. By His grace, He revealed that the two were not mutually exclusive – however, it required surrendering to His way.

In a vision, I saw my brother-in-law standing before God and he was naked. I heard the voice of the Lord say to me, "There are no fig trees in heaven. No one can hide anything from Me."

I knew I could release them and forgive him. In Matthew 18:18 we are told, "Truly, I say to you, whatever you bind on earth shall be bound in heaven, and whatever you loose on earth shall be loosed in heaven". I never understood it.

Of course during our deliverance ministry, we used that Scripture to bind the demons. We would bind them and send them to hell. When we had the next meeting, those same people would be there for deliverance…again! I began to see something was wrong with what we were doing.

As I studied the Scriptures, I saw that Jesus wasn't talking about demons at that time. The chapter was on forgiveness. I learned that if I don't forgive, I can't be forgiven and then I am bound to that person until I do forgive. That day I forgave my brother-in-law; three days later, I read of his death notice in the paper. God had been merciful – He allowed me to forgive this man before he died, so that I am no longer bound by him.

Not only was forgiveness the path to Jean's personal freedom and release, but God's timing was profound. Through this example, and many others, Jean learned that to delay the promptings of God was to miss opportunities for growth and healing – for her and for others. Obedience to God's promptings, though not perfectly followed, became increasingly important.

Jean ministered to many people for many years, but God was faithful to minister to her. As she drew near to Him, He continued to reveal a better way to understand Him and to understand herself.

I have been a pastor, teacher, missionary, radio preacher, and tent evangelist. I've started churches, and I've experienced every kind of witness that there is. My life has been filled with <u>doing the work of God</u>. It took me many, many years to realize I didn't need to be <u>doing</u>, I only needed to <u>be</u>.

Because of Jean's tenuous beginnings – an unwanted birth and abandonment by her father – Jean had low self-esteem, despite her spiritual accomplishments and knowledge. In an attempt to gain God's favor, she applied the earthly tactics of "running and running and doing and doing." Daily she would retreat to her bedroom for prayer, accompanied by her dog and cat. She would fervently pray.

I would ask God continually to answer my prayers. I would come every morning with my laundry listing and go through the list. It took me years to learn that God wanted to speak to me also.

I would fear the Scripture Psalms 46:10 that said, "Be still, and know that I am God. …" I got to the place where I hated that Scripture because the one problem I hated was being still. To "be still" meant you were not doing anything, and of course I wanted to be in control of my life and everyone else's also. Now, my prayer life is so changed!

The absence of a loving father throughout her childhood left a void in Jean that was not readily ignored. Despite her knowledge of the Scripture and communing with God the Father, Jean had a distorted view of all "fathers" on an unconscious level. During a daily meditation, God provided an intimate revelation of the Trinity – Holy Spirit, Jesus the Son, and God the Father. The Holy Spirit and Jesus led her to her loving Father who desired to be with her (and us) – not for what she could *receive* from Him but for what she could experience just *being* in His Presence.

One day in meditation, the Spirit was brooding over me, telling all about Himself and His ministry – how He came to be my Comforter, Guide, Teacher, Counselor; how He convicts of sin; and mostly how He brings us to Jesus. No man can come to Jesus unless the Holy Spirit leads him. As we spent time together, I asked Him if He could lead me to Jesus. He took me by the hand and said, "That's my delight - to bring you to Jesus; that's why I brood over you." Just as He brooded over Mary until the seed of Christ was quickened in her by the Holy Spirit, so it is with us.

Then He brought me to a door (which at the time I didn't understand). He put my hand on the doorknob and opened it – lo and behold, it was Jesus! I remembered John 10:9 where Jesus declares "I am the door. If anyone enters by me, he will be saved and will go in and out and find pasture."

As I went through the Door, I was embraced by my elder brother Jesus, and I saw myself walking down the road to Emmaus. His arms were around my shoulders. Then He began to reveal Himself – just like He did with the disciples after His resurrection.

Remember, He wanted to continue the journey and they wanted to stop and rest for the evening.

Luk 24:13-15, 27-31 That very day two of them were going to a village named Emmaus, about seven miles from Jerusalem, (14) and they were talking with each other about all these things that had happened. (15) While they were talking and discussing together, Jesus himself drew near and went with them.

(27) And beginning with Moses and all the Prophets, he interpreted to them in all the Scriptures the things concerning himself. (28) So they drew near to the village to which they were going. He acted as if he were going farther, (29) but they urged him strongly, saying, "Stay with us, for it is toward evening and the day is now far spent." So he went in to stay with them. (30) When he was at table with them, he took the bread and blessed and broke it and gave it to them. (31) And their eyes were opened, and they recognized him. And he vanished from their sight.

He stayed with them, but He would've gone further. I believe that's where some of us are – Jesus would have us go further. The disciples wanted to have their village, which is where they were more familiar and comfortable. Likewise, it is so hard for us many times to leave the "comfort zone". After awhile, their eyes were opened again.

As I was walking with the Lord, He began explaining what His ministry was to me and to the world. I began to understand that He is my Bread; I'll never hunger (physically, emotionally or spiritually) again. He is the Alpha and the Omega, the beginning of my life and the end of it. In Philippians 1:6 "And

I am sure of this, that he who began a good work in you will bring it to completion at the day of Jesus Christ." I began to see that He was in total control of my life. When He revealed He is the Way, the Truth, and the Life, I knew I didn't have to worry what road to take because He is the Way; as long as I followed Him, I would never go down the wrong path (even if I did, He would be with me). He is the Resurrection; I knew I would never die, but have life and a fuller life than any can ever know!

I also learned He had sent the Holy Spirit to me to guide me into all truth for in Him is no lie (John 16:13). "When the Spirit of truth comes, he will guide you into all the truth, for he will not speak on his own authority, but whatever he hears he will speak, and he will declare to you the things that are to come." I learned that the Holy Spirit will reveal what He hears and disclose it to me! In Revelations 22:16, "'I, Jesus, have sent my angel to testify to you about these things for the churches. I am the root and the descendant of David, the bright morning star.'" Jesus sent his Angel (the Holy Spirit) to reveal Truth. The greatest revelation comes when He reveals His real true purpose to me – He came to be the Pattern Son, our Elder Brother, and our Savior. His greatest purpose was to reveal the Father to not only me, but the whole world!

Because of poor earthly role models, it's difficult for many people to grasp the true meaning of what a loving father is like. In Jean's experience, her father left home when she was three years old; she had no positive concept of what a father was like. When she visited the homes of friends, particularly those with stay-at-home moms and fathers, she would linger around, hoping to be invited to stay for supper. She could not remember sharing a meal with her earthly father, and she longed for that intimate fellowship.

Little did I realize that the desire I had all those years was for my Heavenly Father; I didn't know it! That's why when I hear Him knock at the door of my heart, I run to open the door so He will come and dine with me.

After we fellowshipped more, I asked Jesus, my Brother, to take me to my Father. He grasped my hand and led me up a high mountain. An air of excitement filled my being, for I could already hear the singing of the angelic choir – singing "Holy, Holy, Holy".

Then Jesus and I were brought before a huge throne with every color of the rainbow over it. Such a sight words cannot explain! I saw the 24 elders laying their crowns at His feet, saying, "Holy, Holy, Holy". Jesus then presented me to my Father and said, "Father, I would like you to meet your child, Jean Yanakos. She began following you at an early age."

I heard my Father say, "I know, Son." I saw myself so small and helpless, but I felt these huge Hands of Love pick me up and put me on Father's lap (which I never experienced in true life), and He embraced me. I began to cry and the first words of comfort I heard were, "It's all right." I began to weep even more, and again I heard the comforting words, "It's all right."

I realized I had Father's full attention, so I began to petition for my loved ones. I heard Him gently say to me, "Be still and know that I am God. Just let Me love you." In a little while, Father began to explain to me why I must receive His love – if I don't receive His love, I cannot love anyone else, not even myself. 1 John 4:19, "We love because he first loved us." We cannot love others until we receive His love. In order to give love away, we must first receive that Love. We cannot give to someone else what we ourselves don't have.

It took me some time before I finally rested in Father's arms and totally received that Love. Then Jesus took His place at the right hand of the Father and began to intercede for different ones and different nations. Many times the Scriptures would be quoted, like Matthew 18:19, "Again I say to you, if two of you agree on earth about anything they ask, it will be done for them by my Father in heaven." No wonder Jesus wanted to hear what Father was saying and doing – so He could agree with His Father, and of course, it was done!

When we hear what Jesus is praying (instead of us telling Him what we want Him to do) – when we quietly listen and *agree with Him, then <u>the prayer is answered</u>. It is not up to us, when the answer comes, as far as time is concerned. 1 John 5:19, "We know that we are from God, and the whole world lies in the power of the evil one." My confidence is that He will answer!! Amen! Jesus knows the perfect will of His Father, for they are <u>One</u>.*

Our prayer life can be revolutionized when we take this approach and agree with Jesus as He intercedes daily for us. When I recognize that His thoughts toward me – and everyone else – are only always good, then I can feel the mercy and compassion He has for those that are lost and in bondage. I even begin to understand what it means "missing the mark." For most Christians, we're not in the really "nasty" sin, but simply "missing the mark".

Over the years, God whispered His truth to Jean and revealed to her precious revelations – He taught her that much can be learned from seasoned believers; that above all else, Jesus must be lifted up to draw all men unto Him; that forgiveness is the only way to freedom and new life, and that the Father so longs for those who are His to *be* with Him and to have them learn to hear what He desires so that their prayers might be answered. The Father is always willing to whisper words of truth and revelation to those who sit and listen to Him…because He truly loves His children.

CHAPTER 6

NOT WITHOUT TEARS

The Lord called Jean to "teach, preach and heal", but she learned that she was in need of all three for herself. The teacher was not exempt from being taught! As Jean continued in her ministry, she functioned to the fullness of her understanding of God and the Scriptures. As her intimacy with God deepened, He revealed a better way – for her and for others.

In my early years of ministry, I felt I had all the answers and knew how to pray. As soon as I became a Christian, I began praying for my husband, who at that time was an alcoholic. I would rebuke, bind, and cast out, and things kept getting worse. I could not understand why God was not answering my prayers. After all, I was praying for 2 to 3 hours a day, reading the Scriptures at least an hour a day, fasting often, and ministering to God's people!

After 25 years of doing this, I heard the Voice of God say to me, "You have been praying for the wrong reasons." I was so shocked. Who me? In James 4:3, "You ask and do not receive, because you ask wrongly, to spend it on your passions." Then God began to show me my motives. I wanted my husband saved and delivered so he would be a better husband and love me more – after all, it was all about me! The Lord had said it was not because I didn't want him to go to hell; it was all for my selfish reasons.

I must admit I was a little perturbed that it took so long to show me. In fact, I told Him that! So now I try to wait on God in fear about what and who I'm praying for so the answers come much more quickly.

Jean learned some lessons in very painful ways. Although she had taught on forgiveness and the grace of God for many years, she still struggled to forgive those who had hurt her – physically, emotionally, and spiritually; she harbored a root of bitterness. That bitterness manifested itself as a tumor that weighed over 40 pounds, and Jean looked like she was nine months pregnant! She had a vision that the tumor left her body and fell to the ground, splitting into four pieces. Because of this vision, she believed God for a miraculous healing.

So, being the great woman of faith that I thought I was, I refused to have an operation. Finally, I had to go to the doctor for something else and the doctor wouldn't take care of what I went in for. He kept insisting that I needed to go to the hospital or I was going to die. I was reminded of Psalm 37:23 "The steps of a man are established by the LORD, when he delights in his way." So I said, "Lord, if this is really You (I put forth the craziest fleece I could), let this doctor not charge me anything for the operation." I was sure I was safe. So when I asked the doctor what his fee would be, he looked over his shoulder, and then looked at me and said, "For you, there will be no charge." I still didn't want to yield, and then I felt a hand on my shoulder and heard these words, "I have answered your stupid fleece."

Reluctantly, Jean went to the hospital; the operation took 12 hours because the tumor was entwined on major organs in her body. Jean requested that the doctor save the tumor so she could see it. Three days later during a post-op examination, he brought Jean the tumor. He explained that it had fallen and split into four pieces – precisely what Jean had seen in her vision! Jean began to cry because she felt she had failed God by not letting Him perform a miraculous healing.

I had my follow-up examination a few weeks later and the medical doctor said to me, "Mrs. Yanakos, most people get their own tumors because of bitterness and unforgiveness." When I left that office, I knew I could not afford the luxury of unforgiveness anymore. It was too costly!

Almost 35 years ago, Jean awoke one morning with a high fever and severe pain. She thought she had the flu, and she remained bedfast for three days. On the third day, she took a shower and began to vomit a brownish color.

I said to myself, "Jean, I think you're sick." I drove to my doctor's with such pain that I was driving 10 miles an hour. When I finally got there, my regular doctor wasn't in; I had to wait for an hour and 15 minutes. I thought I was going to die with pain!

Finally, the doctor saw me and said, "You are very sick." I felt like saying, "What gave you the clue?"…but I kept my mouth shut! He said, "You need to get to the hospital." I drove myself to a local emergency room hospital, which was not the right one. As I was crawling out of the car, some nurses saw me and brought a wheelchair for me.

After the initial examination, the doctor left the room. The door was ajar, and Jean heard him say to the nurse, "She's going to die. She'll never make it to the other hospital." When Jean heard that, she began to cry and tell the Lord that if this was His plan, she was ready. The ambulance delivered her to the right hospital; she was operated on for ruptured diverticulitis. All that poison had been in her body for three days.

I was in the hospital for 15 days and then had to go back for another five days because of infections. I knew from my Biblical studies that I had not gotten rid of the garbage that I was carrying – bitterness and unforgiveness. I began to repent again.

In the meantime, I had to wear a colostomy bag for they had to remove 8 inches of my colon, but the encouraging prognosis was that I could have it reversed. I learned so many lessons from wearing that bag for a whole year. I even made missionary trips to Singapore and Hong Kong wearing that bag.

The biggest thing was that I no longer had control of my bodily functions. Whenever my bowels decided to evacuate, no matter on a plane, in a church, in a restaurant, in the car, I had no control! Do you think that was a lesson I needed to learn – not to be in control?!?

I so longed for a certain member of my family to be there for me. I heard these words: "I will give all those you need, but not who you want." The love and care I received from my Christian family was so wonderful, but again, not the one I wanted. I finally repented again. Notice how many times I had to repent! You would think I would have remembered!

A year later, Jean's colostomy was reversed. The doctor said, "We removed your gallbladder which was full of stones. Jean was so grieved in her spirit because she knew what that meant: she still had hardness in her life that she had not completely dealt with. Again, she needed repentance for the hardness and bitterness that she had allowed.

All that junk and garbage had come back into my life. But I thank God that it was done at the time of the reversal of the colostomy. God was merciful to bring it to the surface and let me know that I had more layers to get rid of. One thing I've learned is that we are so very fragile, even from our mother's womb. We have had messages sent to us as children and throughout our lives. I didn't know how to handle them or let go of them. Every time I was abused, rejected, or unloved, I received a scar. So now in my adult life, I can understand why I am so scarred and bruised. I have believed the lie about myself, rather than the truth.

Quite some time ago, I woke up with these words coming out of my mouth: "You were created for loving. You are a gift of love to this world, and I will teach you how to give it away." It took me forever to believe that! First of all, how could I be lovable if my own father left when I was three and my mother was too busy for me? The lie was that I must not be lovable. When I heard those words that I was created for love, it began to make sense to me. I was created in my Father's image.

"Gen 1:26-27 Then God said, "Let us make man in our image, after our likeness. And let them have dominion over the fish of the sea and over the birds of the heavens and over the livestock and over all the earth and over every creeping thing that creeps on the earth." (27) So God created man in his own image, in the image of God he created him; male and female he created them.

I know that God is love. So my Daddy's DNA is love.

From infancy, a baby expresses its need for and dependency upon its parents. Parents provide the necessary nurturing and love for emotional and physical well-being. Various studies have been conducted in orphanages throughout Europe, documenting the necessity of nurturing touch. These children were diapered, given bottles, and deposited on pillows or cribs, providing the physical needs. However many developed physical ailments and even died "for no apparent reason". Scientists indicate that babies need human touch at least 13 to 15 times a day. Some of the babies in Russia became blind or deaf for no physical reasons that could be determined.

So now I understand that there will be no 'lone rangers' in the Kingdom of God. We need each member of the family, both physical and spiritual. We cannot say, "I don't need you."

God's teaching on love helped Jean understand the importance of belonging in the Body of Christ. She gained a deeper appreciation for the need of nurturing one another through prayer, fellowship, and yes, even physical touch. For believers to grow into the fullness of who God created them to be, they need to connect with others on a meaningful level – loving and being loved!

Jean's marriage was not a clear example of loving and being loved; it was a dysfunctional love-hate meshing which brought sorrow, pain, and unconventional support. Strangely, even when Jean finally moved out of their home after her children had grown, her husband helped her move, and often he provided handyman assistance in her new residence.

He could fix anything. If I needed him, I could call him and he would come over and fix things. I just made him a plate of spaghetti, and he was happy. When he was sick, I took care of him. He would come over here and sleep on the couch, and I would take care of him. When I got so sick 18 years ago, I was upstairs in my bed and he was asleep on the couch. I had a little bell and if I needed him, I would ring the bell. He would come up and see what I needed.

So in his way, he loved me as much as anyone could love anybody. He never knew what love was because he never saw that in his own home; he never knew how to respond to love in any way. When he got sick at the end, he was in the hospital and he had cancer of the bladder, prostate, and throat from smoking and drinking. He was 92 years old at this time two years ago, and I went to see him every day when he was in hospital. He said, "You – you're the only one that I want to come now."

When I first became a Christian, he wouldn't let me go to church. He fought it tooth and nail. I wanted to go to church, and I was determined that I was in a good church because that was the only hope I had. I was to go to church and get filled up with the power of God. He would fight me and he would never let me pray if he had a need. He'd say, "Forget it! Go on believing your prayers." He was a very mean man, and yet I know as much as he could love anybody, he loved me more than anybody else.

I would go to see him every day when he was sick at the end and as soon as I would come in he would say, "You're going to pray now?" And I'd say "I'm going to pray." He'd say, "And you're going to ask God to heal me?" And I'd say to him, "I'm going to ask God to bless you with whatever you need." "No, I want you to ask God to heal me. I want to be healed." I said, "Bill, okay. I will pray." When I finished, he would say, "Amen… amen… amen!" It was a funny expression. He passed away two years ago in October.

Women in abusive and alcoholic relationships rarely set healthy boundaries for themselves, and most suffer from low self-esteem. Breaking the bondage of a co-dependent relationship is threatening because the known, even though unsafe, offers a false sense of security in its familiarity. Breaking free from such a relationship is often a process that takes years.

Jean grieved deeply when her husband passed away. He had accepted the Lord as his Savior, yet their relationship was never fully healed of the abuse and injury from their early years together. The sorrow of what could have been and should have been mingled with the loss of the one with whom she had joined her life – perhaps the final resolution will only be seen on the other side. If that relationship with her husband had been fully healed, would she have developed the intense dependency she had on the Lord? Only God knows, nonetheless, she continued to believe that God would work all things together for good – even those which are, as yet, incomplete or unexplainable.

The death of Jean's husband brought deep sorrow and tears, but not all tears are the result of heartache and sadness! Jean had the great honor of officiating at her granddaughter's wedding in Greece in 2009. Her granddaughter and fiancé Elias went out to lunch with Jean and requested that she come to Greece to marry them.

I was kind of shocked because I didn't expect that. And I said, "Well, yes!" She said, "The ceremony is going to be all in Greek. So I have to have my Memaw there to marry me so I'll feel like I'm really married!" How precious! But I thought, "Oh, my! What am I going to say?"

The wedding was scheduled to be held outside. All week it had rained! It was cloudy and cold, and the wind was blowing in off the Mediterranean Sea. Like all brides, her granddaughter longed for a sunny day for her wedding, and she considered it Memaw's assignment to adjust the weather!

The day before the wedding, my granddaughter said, "All right, Memaw, get busy!" The day of the wedding, it was still cold and cloudy, and she said, "Memaw, you don't have too much time left!" We were getting our hair fixed for the wedding, and it was still really cloudy! It was about five o'clock, and the wedding was just about ready to start. She said, "Memaw, you sure are down to the wire!" Would you believe that when the wedding started, the sun came out and it was so beautiful!

During the Greek wedding, the bride and groom did not say anything. The priest talked in Greek, and they walked around in a circle with a crown on their heads. There was so much symbolism! Then it was time for Jean to share words that would hopefully touch the hearts of the bride and groom and their invited guests.

His parents were there, and they were the loveliest people. When I started the ceremony, this is what God gave me. I said, "The greatest gift that my granddaughter could give to her husband is to take his name." Because in Greece, when you get married, your name changes in spelling and the meaning of the name – it shows that you're married. And I said to him, "The greatest gift that you can give to her is your name. By that, you are saying, 'She has my love. I love her more than anyone else. I will provide for her. I will take care of her. I will nurture her.'" His mother was sitting in the front row, and she started nodding to all of her friends in total agreement. She was so pleased with what she was hearing.

Then I thought about that for us. That goes in line with when we become Christians. When we become Christians, we take on Jesus' name and we become "little Christs". That meant a lot to me! Now I know that I have been given His name. I know that I am loved by Him, and He's going to provide for me; He's going to take care of me and He's going to nurture me! So even though the words were meant for them, it was also a lesson for me! It was a beautiful wedding, and she made a beautiful bride!

My granddaughter was touched by the ceremony and the words I said. She started crying because she was so in love with this young man, and she took his name!

Tears can be an expression of sorrow. They can mark the journey of the heart as God patiently and lovingly cleans out the rubbish and wounds that we have accumulated through things we have done or things that have been done to us.

Tears can also be expressions of deep joy. They can be the overflow of experiencing something that deeply satisfies our soul. The journey is not without tears.

CHAPTER 7

FINISHING STRONG

Within 6 to 8 months of attending North Way Christian Community, Jean started to teach Bible classes. The sessions were offered at various times – Sunday mornings, Tuesday mornings, or evening sessions at various locations – and they covered a variety of topics: Growing in Christ, the Holy Spirit, The Phases of Christian Maturity, and The Tabernacle, to name a few.

Even now in her ninth decade of life, Jean continues to conduct formal Bible classes at church and in her home. Some classes are filled to capacity, and at other times, Jean presents instruction one-on-one to a hungry soul. She shares what she has learned to be true over a lifetime of walking with God. She is candid in sharing her past mistakes, in hopes that others can learn from them rather than make the same painstaking errors.

Although Jean mentored a mixed group of singles for several years, most of her teachings and ministry has been to women. Jean can readily relate to women in crisis or challenging situations because of her own life experiences. She has gained a seasoned perspective from a lifetime of walking with God and seeing His faithfulness. Her intimate journey with God and study of His Word enable her to speak life-transforming lessons to the women who have attended her Bible studies.

Jean also conducted women's retreats at an off-site location in Ligonier, Pennsylvania for 18 consecutive years, missing only one year due to some significant health complications. The women who attended were hungry for the Presence of God and the on-going theme became "you will never be the same again".

Throughout these retreats, God manifested His glory and grace with answered prayers, personal words of encouragement, and healings. There were many miracles, and one particular one involved a woman who had an unusual condition – she could not perspire. Initially, this condition would seem to be a blessing, not a curse, but the absence of sweating meant her body was filled with toxins; she was sick all the time.

The woman's daughter had recently become a Christian and was taught to "forsake mother and father and cleave only to God – forget all others!" The mother was distraught at the words which threatened her relationship with her daughter and came to a retreat to find out what this "Christian stuff" was all about. Jean had not presented the distorted teaching of abandoning parents for the sake of God. Nonetheless, because Jean was the authority at the retreat, this woman was coming to check her out and expose the fraudulent teachings!

While I was ministering, she [this woman] was sitting in her seat. Slowly, she slid off the chair and laid down on the ground. I happened to look at her and I said out loud, "Someone is sleeping in the Lord. She must be receiving healing." That was all there was to it.

The next morning she came to me, and she said, "I want you to know what I did. I came here to prove you were a fake, but I got healed last night!" She said, "I have not perspired since I couldn't tell you when, but God healed me!" That was a real miracle! She came to my meetings for years, and then they moved out of town.

At these retreats, God often moved powerfully after a teaching paved the way to a deeper understanding of His truth.

Jean and the other speakers prayerfully sought to be led by the Holy Spirit in their instructions, even discarding prepared teachings if prompted by God. Each session was a stretching experience for the teachers, as well as those receiving the teaching, as the teachers stepped out in faith to follow the promptings of the Holy Spirit.

One other time, Carol (my daughter who was one of my speakers) came to me and said, "Mom, I've got a real hard task – I can't speak on what I was planning." When she told me what she was going to speak on, I about died. I thought, "Oh, my goodness!" because these were all Christian women. She said, "The Lord told me that I'm to deal with molestation." I said, "Well, there will be three of us here – you, me, and the doctor (who was a speaker at the meeting). So if no one else comes up for prayer, at least there will be the three of us there praying." Lo and behold, she made the call about anybody who had been molested to come for prayer, and I think there were 92 women who ran up to the altar. There was such an outpouring of God's love and women getting free! I never saw so many tears in my life!

Carol traveled with me all over the world. Every time I went overseas, she would come and be a speaker, too! It was always very powerful!

People are sometimes skeptical of the power of God or the accuracy of a "word" given from God. Two years ago, God confirmed His participation in a word given to Validia Gloster, a first time attendee at one of the Divine Getaway Retreats. In Validia's words, this is what happened during this time of ministry:

Jean said, "Yolanda! Yolanda! I have need of you!" I got up, then I ran down front. I said, "Here am I. What do you need?" Jean began to speak over my life and share all the things that she saw in me and in my ministry - the gifts that God was going to bestow on me and everything that God was pouring into my spirit - those things yet to come and those things that had already happened. It was just a beautiful pro- phetic word that poured out of her spirit. I went back to my seat and my god-daughter said, "Why did you answer to her when she called you Yolanda?" And I said, "I don't know!" I was not quite sure, but I knew when she called 'Yolanda' that was me! I was sure absolutely - without a doubt.

When I went back to my room, I prayed about it and I said, "Lord, tell me why I answered to Yolanda?" And God reminded me that on my journey, I was raised in a Baptist church; I moved into a neighborhood with my cousins and I became an Episcopalian for while; my other cousins were going to St. Kinesis Catholic Church and I decided I wanted to become Catholic because they could go to church on Friday (then I didn't have to go to church on Saturday and Sunday and I could hang out). When I was at St. Kinesis and going through the catechism, I chose the name 'Yolanda'. I had chosen that as my catechism name because Martin Luther King's daughter's name was Yolanda and he called her 'Yogi' for short. I thought that was absolutely fabulous and I wanted to be called Yogi, so if they made that my catechism name, I would be known as Validia Marie Yolanda Gloster – they could call me 'Yogi' for short.

God brought that all back to my remembrance! Immediately when I saw Pastor Jean the next morning I said to her, "Let me tell you the confirmation of the Holy Spirit and why you called me Yolanda!"

Jean has often shared that no one is more amazed than she is when such a word is confirmed. It's always a "leap of faith" to proclaim a "word" to someone – if she's wrong, she looks foolish; if she's right, she realizes that she *has* heard from God's heart and it's very humbling! Always it relies upon the leading of the Holy Spirit!

A few years ago, the leaders at North Way asked Jean to teach the youth group about the Holy Spirit. The gap in age between this octogenarian and the teens was not a deterrent; Jean's no nonsense, straight-talking delivery seemed to be the perfect format for these young people.

Jean accepted the request; she was eager to plant the seeds for unleashing God's power in these young Christians.

Accompanied by Scott Stevens (then Associate pastor), she conducted a brief class. Being a teacher who encourages practical application, she then invited the students to respond by seeking prayer.

At first no one was responding. First one – then another – then the next thing we knew there were 70 or more swarming us – all wanting prayer! They began speaking in tongues like you couldn't believe! I yelled to Scott, "Scott, come over here and pray!" He would say, "I've got someone to pray with over here!" Some of the youth leaders came for prayer and received the Holy Spirit, too. It was amazing!! Some of those kids went on a mission trip to Nicaragua. That's where they got inundated with the Holy Spirit and fire!!

Jean has remained active, not only in her spiritual training, but also in her physical training, working out at Club Julian, a local health spa, three times a week. She has four different personal trainers depending upon the day of her attendance and their scheduled work. When she meets up with her personal trainer, there are often other spa attendees who follow her workout circuit to glean from the teachings, personal experiences, and insights that she shares while she works out. She regularly chats with a Lutheran pastor, and she gave him notes for her teaching on the Holy Spirit. More recently she told him the story of the street car fare [see Chapter 2].

He said, "Can I use your story about the quarter?" I said, "Yes!" He said that his church is hurting right now because of the economy. I said, "Well, you know people don't really know how to tithe. They're afraid of giving the 10% or whatever because they're fearful about money – they wonder how they are going to live." He said, "That's right." I said, "That little story is one of the reasons why I've never been afraid to give liberally. If you see what I give compared to my income, you'd say, 'How can she do that?' because it never matches. I love to give, and I have a great love for the missionaries."

Then I started talking to a Catholic priest. He said, "I hear we're in the same business." And I said, "Yes." He said, "That's wonderful! They tell me that you've traveled a great bit." I said,

"Well, I've traveled some, and I've had retreats for men and women." It was a joy to talk with such an honest, young man.

One of Jean's personal trainers was hospitalized, and she made a visitation, complete with a quart of homemade chicken noodle soup. She prayed for him and reminded him of the grace and love of God. Promoting health and wholeness of the body and the spirit are never separate issues!

In her personal Bible study and reading, Jean continues to delight in Scriptures that God quickens to her understanding. During a personal time of reading in the Psalms, God enlightened her understanding regarding a particular Psalm.

I love David's writings! Psalm 92: 12-15 was given to me on February 13, 2010:

Psa 92:12-15 The righteous flourish like the palm tree and grow like a cedar in Lebanon. (13) They are planted in the house of the LORD; they flourish in the courts of our God. (14) They still bear fruit in old age; they are ever full of sap and green, (15) to declare that the LORD is upright; he is my rock, and there is no unrighteousness in him.

I knew the Lord was telling me that here I am 88 and I'm still going to begin to have fruit; I'm going to flourish like a palm tree! When you see the palm tree with all the dates on it and how those dates fall down, they are so wonderful! When you get a date from a palm tree, they are the sweetest! He says, "You shall flourish… you shall bear fruit in old age." I jumped on that, and I said, "Okay, Lord, I believe that!"

I'm seeing that now in my classes. I have a class here in my home on Thursday nights. I make it a habit that at nine o'clock we are done because some of them are working women. I feel like they need to go home and get to bed so they can get up and go to work. They'll say, "No! No! Don't stop! Keep going! Keep going!" And I say, "No, you need your rest. I'm going to quit."

So I quit…right on the dot…so they can go home and get their rest. It's wonderful to see people saying, "Please don't stop, please don't stop." It's because there's such a hunger. This is the time now that God wants to minister to those who are hungry. I believe we are on the verge of something so supernatural that it will astound the world. I'm excited, but I still stay true to what I say – at nine o'clock, we're done!

In the past month, Jean has led three young men to the Lord. Her past ministry has most frequently been to women, but now, for whatever reason, God has brought young men into her path. Undaunted by the shift, Jean shares the Gospel with them in her typical frankness and candor. The end result is that they embrace Christ as Savior. Clearly, a life of experiencing God's faithfulness gives credibility to her words, words that are worth sharing. Because of that rich reservoir of experience and knowledge, those who have benefited from Jean's teaching in the past started requesting that she have a retreat.

Everybody's been after me to have another retreat – have another retreat! At the last retreat we had, I was very weak. I had gone through a siege of weakness like I had never had. I was unable to really preach because I was so weak, and so my daughter had to take over most of the retreat. I would gather strength to give a few words to people, but then I would have to sit down. That happened to me a couple times when I was in Singapore.

When I was in Singapore I had such exhaustion because I had prayed for 500 people at one meeting. I had to go to the hospital, and the doctor said, "This woman can't go home. She has to stay here." I couldn't afford to buy another plane ticket; I had a ticket already purchased. I said, "I can't stay another day. I have to leave tomorrow." And he said, "You can't. I will not be responsible for you." I said, "Please, I have got to go home; I've got to go." He saw that I was determined, so he said to my daughter, "Will you make sure she goes to the doctor as soon as she gets home?" My daughter said, "She will." I got home, and I went to the doctor. The next day they put me in the hospital; I stayed there for about five days until I got my strength back.

So when they asked me to have a new retreat, I said, "I can't have another retreat. I can't take it anymore because when ministering, I minister with my whole body." It takes every bit of strength when the power of God goes through me.

Jean knew the benefits of past retreats. Even though her age had diminished her strength and stamina, she was still willing to be used of God to minister to others. She inquired about availability of the previous location for retreats, Antiochian Village in Ligonier, Pennsylvania. The charge for staying at the retreat facility had increased significantly; the higher price would be cost prohibitive for many of the women. Jean considered that door closed.

With additional inquiries, Jean found that there was space available at North Way Christian Community, her home church, for Friday evening and Saturday morning. The location was convenient, the retreat time was less than a typical weekend retreat (accommodating her limited stamina), and the cost would be greatly reduced. The Divine Getaway Retreat was scheduled for August 26 and 27, 2011, open to both men and women.

Jean sought God for His word for this specific conference; she prayed daily, long into the night – sometimes all night – seeking His leading. By His direction, she planned to teach on Entering into a Relationship with the Holy Spirit.

I've been doing this for 66 years and you would think I would know how to have a service – but every night I would go to bed and say, "Lord, how are we going to start the service? What do You want me to say? What Scriptures should I use?" And nothing would come. I would say, "Lord, if you don't show up, nothing's going to happen. It's just going to be a dead meeting!" I didn't want that! You'd think I had never led a meeting before! I've been praying and praying and praying. Then I'd wake up at three in the morning and I'd hear the Lord speaking to me and saying, "This is what I want you to do…"

The meeting opened with refreshing praise and worship. Those in attendance were encouraged to give to God the same exuberant expressions of awe and admiration that they would bestow on a president, king or sports star. Jean then encouraged attendees to reflect upon Amos 3:7 and 8.

Amo 3:7-8 "For the Lord GOD does nothing without revealing his secret to his servants the prophets. (8) The lion has roared; who will not fear? The Lord GOD has spoken; who can but prophesy?"

One of the gifts that God has given me is the gift of prophecy. But I would like to say that in a different way. Prophecy can come in many, many different ways. If you've ever been in my class, you know that everybody can prophesy. To prophesy means you edify, you encourage, and you comfort. Can anybody do that? Can you do that? Everybody can prophesy because everybody can encourage, everybody can edify, and everybody can comfort somebody.

I went to Giant Eagle on Wednesday and there was a little woman with white hair. She was dressed beautifully and I couldn't keep my eyes off her. I watched her shopping and she had arms about half the size of mine.

Finally, I couldn't stand it. I went over to her I said, "You know what - you look absolutely beautiful!" She had on a very nice outfit. And she started crying. I have that effect on people. And she said, "Oh, I needed to hear that so badly!" And I said, "Why. She said, "I had a big fight with my daughter and she told me that I don't know what I am doing." I said, "How old are you?" She said, "92." And I said to her, "You tell your daughter when she gets to be 92, she won't be half as good as you are!" She said, "Thank you so much! I needed to hear that so badly!"

I was prophesying to her and she didn't even know it. I said to her finally, "Can I say little prayer for you?" And she said, "Would you?" I did and I said, "Don't go home and fight with your daughter. Just go home and say 'Someone told me that I'm pretty today.'" She just thought I was some old lady but I do that because I believe everybody needs to be encour-

aged. Everybody needs to know that they are somebody and that they are loved of God.

Jean admonished all those attending the retreat to make room for the Holy Spirit so that they might experience the freedom and the power to live a life reflecting all of God's grace and goodness. She invited those present to come forward for prayer and gave many "words" that specifically touched the individuals receiving them. Prophecy was present in natural and supernatural ways!

Jean continues to share the Gospel with the same fervor that she demonstrated in the early years of her Christian walk. Her perspective is different – wiser, more confident in her Provider, yet still deeply passionate about the rich teachings God has imparted over the years. Recently God revealed to her a word for the Church regarding these current times starting with Isaiah 40:15:

> Isa 40:15 Behold, the nations are like a drop from a bucket, and are accounted as the dust on the scales; behold, he takes up the coastlands like fine dust.

Do you know how much Japan has moved after the tsunami of 2011? 8 feet!

> Isa 40:17-22 All the nations are as nothing before him, they are accounted by him as less than nothing and emptiness. (18) To whom then will you liken God, or what likeness compare with him? (19) An idol! A craftsman casts it, and a goldsmith overlays it with gold and casts for it silver chains. (20) He who is too impoverished for an offering chooses wood that will not rot; he seeks out a skillful craftsman to set up an idol that will not move. (21) Do you not know? Do you not hear? Has it not been told you from the beginning? Have you not understood from the foundations of the earth?

Then I thought, wow!

Isa 40:22-23 It is he who sits above the circle of the earth, and its inhabitants are like grasshoppers; who stretches out the heavens like a curtain, and spreads them like a tent to dwell in; (23) who brings princes to nothing, and makes the rulers of the earth as emptiness.

And that's what we've seen happening. There in Libya, another uprising in Yemen and people are fighting. They are trying to get rid of their leaders.

Isa 40:24 Scarcely are they planted, scarcely sown, scarcely has their stem taken root in the earth, when he blows on them, and they wither, and the tempest carries them off like stubble.

Rom 14:11 for it is written, "As I live, says the Lord, every knee shall bow to me, and every tongue shall confess to God."

I don't know how it's going to happen, but I know God's going to do it.

And God gave me a vision: I saw a huge cauldron. It was bubbling up like apple butter does when it's cooking. If you've ever seen apple butter cooking, it bubbles up real slow and easy. As I was watching, I saw the nations being thrown into the caldron. They were pink – kind of like a heart. Then I saw this huge wooden spoon that was stirring the cauldron. Then I saw the nations lined up like dominoes. Have you ever seen kids play with dominoes and then line them all up? The first will fall and all the rest of them fall. That's what I saw. I saw all of these nations lined up and then being thrown down one by one. I said to myself, "I wonder what nations they are?" He spoke and said one was Libya and the last one to fall will be Syria.

The Lord spoke to me and said, "These people are rebel-ling against the kings that they have. They're looking for a new king, and they don't realize that it's the King of Kings that they're looking for." So all of these nations are as a drop in the bucket. The Lord said, "Tell the Church that they never need to be afraid of what's going on." God is in total control. Did you hear me? I will never be afraid because He said in Philippians 1:7, "It is right for me to feel this way about you all, because I hold you in my heart, for you are all partakers with me of grace, both in my imprisonment and in the defense and confirmation of the gospel." That ought to encourage you never to allow the devil to bring fear to you about what's going to happen.

I heard in my spirit the word of the Lord saying, "This is of me." In other words, God was causing all of this disruption. He said, "What the devil meant for evil, I am going to turn around for good if the church begins to seek My face and do what is in the Scripture: Matthew 6:33, "But seek first the kingdom of God and his righteousness, and all these things will be added to you."

Everything that we need is going to be added so that we will be able to do the work of God. The people of God never need to be afraid of what's going on. God is in total control. He said, "I hold you in the palm of My hand and none of your enemies can move you out of My hand!" So never allow fear to come to you about what is going to happen. He said that He is going to bring about one of the greatest revivals we've ever seen.

It's a passionate word – one worthy of heartfelt consid-eration and reflection. This is a word birthed from a woman past the normal childbearing years, yet a woman who is still bearing "children" for God.

This child of God still desired confirmation regarding the writing of this book, and she shared that Habakkuk 2:2-3 con-firmed the importance of completing this project:

Hab 2:2-3 And the LORD answered me: "Write the vision; make it plain on tablets, so he may run who reads it. (3) For still the vision awaits its appointed time; it hastens to the end—it will not lie. If it seems slow, wait for it; it will surely come; it will not delay.

Jean Yanakos has walked with God for almost nine decades, and in that time God Almighty has shown Himself faithful time and time again. She has been a conduit of His power and grace, not because of her spiritual abilities, but because of His! Jean did not have great faith, and she did not have the perfect life. What she did have was a deep hunger for God and a willingness to follow after Him, even when she wasn't sure where He would take her or what He would ask her to do.

God chooses to manifest His gifts and love through "earthen vessels", and in the process of using His "earthen vessels", He continues to refine and love the vessel, too! Because of God's faithfulness and abounding grace, Jean has gone the distance and is finishing strong.

If He has done that for her, can He not do the same for you?

Praying Before the Retreat

Smiling with Divine Anticipation

Exhorting Retreat Participants

Praising God with the Tambourine

Reading the Scriptures

Teaching and Preaching

Delivering a Word from God

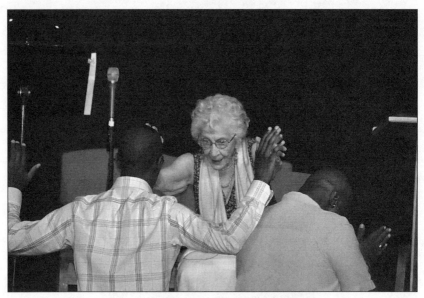

Laying On Hands of Blessing

Sharing More Words of Encouragement

Loving on her "Armor Bearer"

Preparing for Another Retreat Day

Expounding on the Revelation

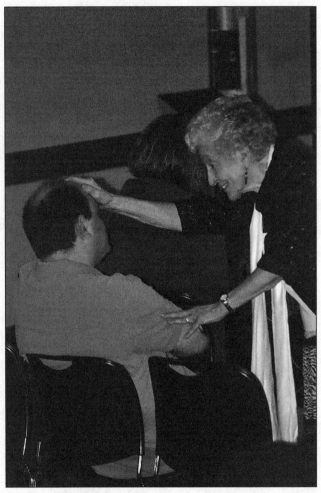

Sharing a Word of Knowledge

"You will never be the same!"

Speaking the Truth in Love

Teaching on the Holy Spirit

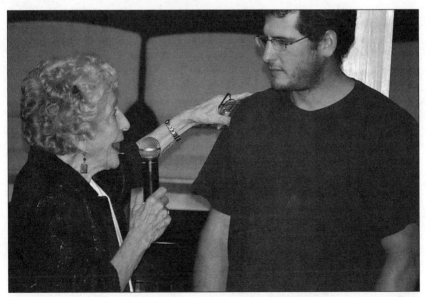

Giving Another Word to a Mentee

Offering Prayers of Gratitude

Rejoicing in God's Goodness

Eye Hath Not Seen…

Blessings to Each One of YOU!